Helping Children Live
with
Death and Loss

Dinah Seibert
Judy C. Drolet
Joyce V. Fetro

Southern Illinois University Press
Carbondale and Edwardsville

06   05   04   03   4   3   2   1

Portions of this book were first published in *Are You Sad Too? Helping Children Deal
with Loss and Death,* copyright © by Dinah Seibert, Judy C. Drolet, and Joyce V. Fetro
(Santa Cruz: ETR Associates, 1993).

Library of Congress Cataloging-in-Publication Data
Seibert, Dinah.
    Helping children live with death and loss / Dinah Seibert, Judy C.
    Drolet, Joyce V. Fetro.
        p. cm.
    Includes bibliographical references.
        1. Children and death. 2. Thanatology. 3. Bereavement in
        children. 4. Loss (Psychology) in children. 5. Children —
        Counseling of. I. Drolet, Judy Catherine, date. II. Fetro,
        Joyce V. III. Title.
BF723.D3 S563 2003
155.9'37'083—dc21
ISBN 0-8093-2464-4 (paper : alk. paper)   2002018701

Printed on recycled paper. ♻

The paper used in this publication meets the minimum requirements of American National
Standard for Information Sciences—Permanence of Paper for Printed Library Materials,
ANSI Z39.48-1992. ∞

To all adults who have the courage to confront their own
attitudes and beliefs toward death and loss and to share
them with children in their lives.

To all children encouraged by these adults to develop a
healthy attitude toward death and loss and a
positive attitude toward everything life has to teach.

Contents

Preface ix
Acknowledgments xiii

Introduction: Educating Children about Death
and Loss 1

1. Reviewing Your Personal History of Death
   Experiences 9

2. Understanding How Children Learn
   about Death 27

3. Learning What Children Need to Know
   about Death 43

4. Answering Children's Questions 59

5. Responding to a Recent Death or Loss 71

6. Using Planned Learning Strategies and Children's
   Literature 95

Glossary 125
References and Additional Readings 129

Preface

People who face the challenge of dealing directly with death and loss often find strengths within themselves that they never knew existed. They may discover that they are truly up to the challenge. They may realize that personal growth can change their perspectives about death and add meaning to their lives. Having witnessed this personal growth in ourselves, friends, loved ones, and students, we developed a commitment to education about death and loss. Our combined history and professional experiences convinced us that this topic is so important it must be shared and explored.

As you read, you'll find that the foundation of our research comes from classic sources because they withstand the test of time very well. Our references and additional readings, however, are updated to include resources with more current examples, applications, and illustrations.

Because we know that children can learn to understand death, because we have respect for their capacity to be resilient and face difficult experiences, and because we know that children can experience the benefits of personal growth, we believe that death education should be shared with children as well as adults. Indeed, in this time of increased mass media reporting of school violence and terrorism close to home, all children potentially are at risk for feeling a major loss in their sense of safety and security. Even when events reported by the media don't affect children directly, indirectly they are affected by being forced into a new reality that "it could happen here" and "it could happen to me." Caring adults must be prepared to provide the education and support children need as they attempt to incorporate this new view into their world.

Since our professional approaches always have emphasized practical applications of concepts through teaching and writing, this book was a natural and exciting step. As we thought about the purpose of this book, we decided on these goals:

- To help parents, teachers, and caregivers become more comfortable with acknowledging death and loss;
- To give adults permission to talk directly to children about death and loss;
- To encourage adults to help children learn the important lessons about life that loss teaches; and
- To provide adults with a practical guide with manageable steps that can be adapted to a variety of situations and stages of growth.

We hope that when you finish this book you will know what we know—that the process of sharing our death and loss experiences helps us cope with the immediate situations and learn lessons for a healthier future. The lessons we learn encompass the breadth of human experience from the specific aspects of coping skills to broader concepts of spirituality. The simple acts of sharing our feelings, beliefs, and knowledge with children nourish the spirits of all of us—adults and children alike. As we share with children, they learn to share with us. We *all* improve our life skills, our compassion, and our inner strengths, which leads to a high level of self-actualization through expanding our spiritual insights.

As we continue to face our own losses, we are reminded that death is not only a natural part of life but also a powerful teacher of the precious gifts we have to offer each other in life. We appreciate this opportunity to share our gifts with you.

Sharing death and loss experiences supports us emotionally and spiritually during difficult times the way a snowshoe supports our weight over deep snow. If all of our body weight is placed on one foot as we step into deep snow, we either fall through and get stuck or our steps are dragged down by the heaviness of the snow. But when our weight is spread over the area of a snowshoe, we are able to keep walking across the top of the snow almost unhindered. We can move forward into new realms of experience and understanding.

If we try to bear a death or loss alone, we may find the weight too great to carry. We may be unable to cope with the daily challenges involved. But when we share the weight of our difficult tasks and emotions with others, it is easier to bear hardships and find ways to cope with our losses.

If we are open to sharing our death and loss experiences with the culturally diverse populations all around us, we grow even further. We have the opportunity to extend our knowledge, understanding, and acceptance as we encounter perspectives different from our own.

We hope that our book can help you to find snowshoes that will carry you and your children through your losses to a fuller understanding of life.

Acknowledgments

Because this book has been stirring in us for such a long time, listing all those who had an influence on its evolution is difficult. Probably many people in our past moved us toward this goal when we weren't even aware of it. Thus, some of our acknowledgments are general, but all are quite sincere.

First, a thank you to the Southern Illinois University Press staff for recognizing the need for this book. We appreciate their support in its production. Special thanks to our acquisitions editor, Elizabeth Brymer, for her expert technical assistance, to Christine Stetter for illustrations that enhance the themes of the text, and to Kathleen Kageff, our copyeditor, for helping us to clarify critical concepts.

We offer our appreciation to all the children and adults who have shared their experiences with us; SIU Carbondale health education students; and friends who listened, shared their experiences, and broadened ours. Our thanks go especially to Dr. Robert Russell, professor emeritus of health education at SIUC, who was an early mentor in death education for us all. Through his courses, his friendship, and teamwork, he provided a foundation in the concepts of death education. He led us to the understanding that death education is really life education.

Our final thanks go to our families, who supported us professionally and personally so that we could take the steps to write this book. They provided the nurturing environment we needed for our past explorations and encouraged us in the effort to share our experience and knowledge with others.

Helping Children Live
with
Death and Loss

Introduction:
Educating Children
about Death and Loss

The Case for Death Education
Understanding What Is Appropriate to Teach
Four Areas of Death Education
How to Use This Book
Beginning

Death and loss are natural parts of life for children as well as adults. Children are not immune to loss. Their experiences range from a friend moving away to a cartoon character getting flattened to a pet dying to their parents divorcing to the death of a loved one. Their reactions to death and loss are as broad as their experiences. How do we know? Because they have questions.

When given the opportunity and a caring and open environment, children ask a broad variety of questions about death. They develop important life skills through reacting and questioning. They practice using the language and feeling the feelings on their way to mastering coping skills. It's up to parents and teachers to provide opportunities and a nurturing environment where children can practice these skills and learn to see death as a natural part of life.

You're not alone if you don't feel ready or prepared for this responsibility. Neither parents, other caregivers, nor teachers are likely to have had preparation for dealing with the subject of death. Death is one of the taboo topics in our society; thus, it is normal to feel uncomfortable talking about death.

Preparing to talk about death and loss means gaining knowledge and becoming comfortable with your feelings. An understanding of biological death is important. But possibly more important is an understanding of the language, traditions, rituals, religious beliefs, and feelings associated with death. It's important to take time to explore your own experiences, spirituality, and feelings before you are in the midst of a death-related crisis. Then you will be able to reflect more objectively.

A personal awareness of death and loss will help you become more comfortable in encouraging children to explore these subjects. There is no good time to lose a loved one. You can't fully prepare for the grief you will experience. But you can learn coping skills to make the grief more bearable. Once you have acknowledged your own feelings and beliefs, you will be more comfortable addressing the topic when children in your life have questions.

As you become more comfortable talking about death and loss, however, you may notice that people around you become *uncomfortable*. They may even label you as "morbid" or "strange." Or they may just avoid discussing the topic with you. Because of this indirect pressure to keep quiet, it takes a special strength and determination to prepare yourself to encourage and support children as they explore death and loss.

This book is written to help you and the children you care about learn more about life by talking about death and loss. We'll show how death education for children can become life education for everyone involved. Coping with death and loss is a life skill that must be taught and nurtured.

The Case for Death Education

Learning and sharing experiences about death and loss aren't easy tasks. So it's important for you to be clear about why death education is a good idea for children. Part of the taboo of death is seen in the way well-meaning adults attempt to shield children from death. In his article "Explaining Death to Children: The Healing Process," Garanzini (1987) makes this dramatic case in favor of sharing death experiences with children:

> Attempts to shield children from the reality of death reinforces in them the perception that death is either not real, too frightening to examine or, worst of all that the ending of life is not worth noting with respect and reverence. These unintended lessons are unhealthy. . . . For the sake of a healthy [and] sound appreciation of the meaning of death, parents and teachers must face the topic realistically and naturally—for themselves and for the children they teach. (30)

The confusion and isolation caused by shielding children from important life events, like death and loss, create an unhealthy stress that can interrupt their growth and development. When these issues are acknowledged and dealt with directly, however, children are able to observe role models, practice coping skills, and learn fully from *all* of their life experiences.

Without an adult to listen, explain, and comfort a child, life lessons are not simply lost—they may be harmful. Children are "excellent observers," but "poor interpreters" (Garanzini 1987, 30). A child's imagination often is much worse than the reality. If you don't talk about death, children will find this absence mysterious and make up a reason for your silence. Suppose a child gets incorrect information from an influential television show. How will the child be able to see the reality or straighten out the facts without an encouraging, direct, and honest adult interpreter? Your role as parent, caregiver, teacher, or interpreter is to use the child's daily life experiences to help teach life skills, including coping with death and loss.

With your help, in small steps, children can learn to express and share their grief. Little by little, they can come to understand that death and loss are natural parts of life, thus mastering an important life skill.

The case for death education for children is clear. In educating children about death and loss, parents and teachers:

- acknowledge and share children's feelings;
- prevent the often unintended but potentially harmful side-effects of ignoring children's interest in death; and
- promote positive emotional development by giving children the ability to cope with even the most difficult aspects of life.

Understanding What Is Appropriate to Teach

The goal of this book is to help you present a positive view of death and loss in your interactions with children. To help you do this we have drawn on a broad background of research as well as personal and professional experiences to help you prepare for talking to children about death and loss. In this book you will find the foundation you need, including:

- terms most often used;
- stages children go through as they develop their ideas about death and loss;
- ways that children experience death and loss; and
- influences on children's perceptions of death and loss.

When you talk to children about death and loss, it is important that you present a positive view of death. But what does that mean?

A positive presentation of death and loss

- is factually accurate,
- is appropriate for the child's level of understanding, and

• creates a healthy understanding of death as a natural part of life rather than one that promotes fear and misunderstanding.

Before you can determine what is appropriate for the child's level of understanding, you must learn how that understanding changes with experience and age. Children's concepts of death become increasingly more detailed, realistic, and factual over time. They move from the view that death is temporary, reversible, and happens only to others to the understanding that death is final, irreversible, and happens to everyone. These different levels of understanding translate into very different interests and questions about death. Once you know how to assess children's abilities, you can move on to deciding what is appropriate teaching material.

Four Areas of Death Education

Death education occurs in both informal and formal ways. It is important for adults to share their feelings and beliefs with children. And the feelings and beliefs of children must be shared, explored, and accepted. Matters such as causes of death and funeral and burial rituals ought to be explained honestly and directly. Finally, children need role models and adult support as they learn skills for coping with death and loss.

For death education to be most beneficial, however, children eventually will need to deal with four important areas in the course of their exploration: *facts, feelings, beliefs, and coping skills.* As a parent or teacher responding to a current death or loss, you may choose to focus on only one of these four areas. Chapter 3 will give you more details about what children need to know about death. If you are a teacher planning a thorough death education curriculum, you will want to include lessons in all four areas.

How to Use This Book

All significant adults in a child's life may become involved with death education experiences. Whether you're the parent, caregiver, teacher, minister, neighbor, relative, or friend, this book is designed for you.

Children are experiencing death and loss regularly. Their experiences may range from changing schools to the death of a bug or a flower to a parent becoming disabled or even the death of a loved one. When children experience loss, they're getting practice at bearing unpleasant feelings like the ones that occur when they experience a death.

So far, we've been talking about ideal situations where planning allows lessons to be given at a pace everyone can manage. A much more common situation occurs when a child either acts out or asks questions in response to an actual death or loss. This is a classic example of "the teachable moment," when parents, caregivers, and teachers must be prepared to focus on whatever aspects are on the minds of the children. Providing immediate emotional support is usually the most important task. But if the children are asking factual questions instead of struggling with emotions, then direct, factual answers are needed. Sometimes professional help is needed. Learning to distinguish between situations you can handle and situations where you need help is most important.

Although the time frame and the intensity will vary, the process of grieving and adjusting to a new life situation is the same for any death or loss. Even small losses, like wilting flowers or torn teddy bears, can teach children big lessons when there is a respectful adult who will listen, explain, and comfort. Whatever their experiences, children are learning from them. With supportive adult interpreters, children can grow and learn powerful lessons. They learn that they can bear unpleasant experiences and survive difficult situations (Furman 1978). What an amazing life gift to give your children.

Parts of the book, such as chapter 5, "Responding to a Recent Death or Loss," is directed more toward parents and caregivers, while chapter 6, "Using Planned Learning Strategies and Children's Literature," are directed primarily toward teachers. Try not to be limited by the phrasing of ideas presented. Think about the concepts and ways to adapt the materials for use in your specific situation. As you read, you'll find suggestions for adults in a variety of roles.

We believe you'll get the most out of this book if you read it completely before putting the ideas into action. When you have the foundation and the "big picture," return to the book to use individual sections and suggestions as you need them.

Chapter 1 walks you through a personal assessment of your own experiences, feelings, and beliefs related to death and loss. Use this self-assessment to prepare yourself emotionally and personally for your work with children. Also, this section will help you become comfortable with the language and concepts used in death education, allowing you to create and maintain the open, accepting environment children need.

In chapter 2, you will learn how children develop their understanding of death in different stages and the characteristics of each stage. This chapter also examines various cultural, social, and religious influences that inform and shape children's views of death.

Chapter 3 describes what children need to know about death. It is divided into the four areas: facts, feelings, beliefs, and coping skills. After this background, you'll find ways to explore each of the four areas and ways to decide which area is most appropriate for your specific situation. This chapter also provides a broad range of ideas to incorporate in a formal death education program.

Chapter 4 provides guidelines for discussing death and loss with children and examples of questions children may ask. The sample answers provided model concepts discussed throughout this book.

Chapter 5 offers support and suggestions for what to do if a death or loss occurs in the lives of your children. It includes discussion of the stages of grief and points to consider in your responses. Then detailed, specific responses are offered for a variety of situations, ranging from the loss a toy to the death of a parent.

In chapter 6, you will find suggestions for implementing planned learning strategies about death and specific activities to use. This section is organized around the four areas described in chapter 3.

If you want to use children's literature to help you teach about death and loss, chapter 6 also provides guidance in selecting appropriate books to use. You'll explore and assess critical factors that will help you select a book that is appropriate for the children's developmental levels as well as the specific situation and needs.

If you've exhausted the contents of this book or you're interested in more detail on a specific concept, see the references and additional readings list at the end of the book. This section documents all research referred to in this book. The glossary at the end of the book provides definitions of various terms used in the book.

Beginning

As you begin your exploration of death and loss as a natural part of life, be alert to the positive messages below. These messages are woven throughout this book, tying positive views of death to positive and healthy emotional development in children.

It is important for adults to help children explore death and loss concepts because:

- death is a natural part of a child's life;
- coping with death is a critical life skill;
- children have questions about death;
- ignoring or denying death is unhealthy; and
- acknowledging death is healthy.

Before you begin sharing your knowledge, feelings, and beliefs about death and loss with children, be sure to:

- understand that children learn about death and loss in small steps over time;
- recognize influences on your own perceptions of death; and
- identify the numerous influences on children's perceptions of death.

Finally, when helping children explore death and loss concepts, it is important to:

- use the child's daily experiences;
- create an open environment where the topic of death is as comfortable as possible;
- use direct, factual language;
- acknowledge and accept children's feelings and beliefs;
- avoid judgment;
- include children in death-related rituals or ceremonies as their interest and understanding allows; and
- revisit death-related experiences with children as they progress through various levels of understanding.

1
Reviewing Your Personal History of Death Experiences

How Do You Feel about Death?
Activity: Finding Death in Daily Life
Activity: Cultural Traditions and Religious or Spiritual Beliefs
Activity: Your Experiences with Loss
Activity: Personal Experiences with Death
Activity: Thinking about Your Own Death
The Next Step

The first step in helping children cope with death and loss is to create a welcoming and open environment where children's feelings and questions are accepted—where death is not a hidden topic. When you feel afraid or incompetent to respond to children's feelings, children quickly learn not to express these feelings openly. If you answer their questions with whispers or with anger, children learn not to ask them. Although not always able to explain their reactions, children are quick to realize when they are making adults uncomfortable. When adults are uncomfortable, children typically don't feel free to explore concepts in their normally expressive and questioning manner.

Since death and loss are extremely personal life situations, you are sharing your own beliefs, experiences, and feelings when you discuss death. You may not *plan* to share your personal history, and you may not be *aware* that you are expressing personal attitudes, but you need to know that your *are.* The way life and death have affected you will influence the way you respond to children's beliefs, experiences, and feelings.

Before you can help children explore their concepts of death and loss, you must explore your own beliefs and biases stemming from your family background and culture, your history with death and loss, and your specific experiences. As you explore each concept, you'll begin to understand its impact on your feelings and actions related to death.

Beliefs

Looking at your beliefs about life after death and funeral rituals will help you see how your religious or spiritual or nonreligious background contributes to an attitude about what happens or should happen when someone dies. Having a specific bias or cultural perspective is neither a strength nor a weakness; it is simply a fact. Being *aware* of your own perspectives and the diversity of perspectives in your community is a strength.

Parent, caregiver, and teacher roles in the area of belief will differ, of course. Because beliefs related to death come from very personal religious, spiritual, and cultural backgrounds, the role of a parent is to teach and reinforce personal beliefs and values. But because classrooms include children from a broad variety of religious, spiritual, and cultural backgrounds, the role of a teacher is to teach and accept the variety of beliefs and values—that is, let children explore freely and encourage them to find out more about what their caregivers, their parents, their teachers, and others believe. The role of a caregiver varies depending on the specific relationship between the child and caregiver. Caregivers who are relatives or parent surrogates will act more like parents. Caregivers who are day care staff will act more as teachers. An in-depth look at your own personal beliefs will prepare you to teach children regardless of your specific role in their lives.

Experiences

While exploring your experiences with death and loss, you'll recall that these experiences have had both positive and negative influences on your attitudes, feelings, and actions. A negative experience with death may have left you fearful, angry, or cynical. As a result, you may deny your feelings, carry your anger into other, inappropriate situations, or isolate yourself from people by putting down their views.

Positive experiences may help you to share positive feelings, direct your hurtful feelings appropriately, and make room for others with opposing views who might present a more positive, hopeful, and healthy perspective. A positive experience is one where new strengths are found. You may find this strength in new skills, new facts, or stronger relationships. Only when you take a hard look into your own past can you see both the negative influences that may have held you back and the positive influences that have helped you grow.

Feelings

Your past feelings have important lessons to teach, too. The simple act of remembering your own powerful emotions, like pain or joy, can remind you to be respectful of other people's feelings. It's useful to try to recall the powerful feelings aroused by death and loss experiences when you're alone and able to reflect on them. Then, the strong feelings from your past will be less likely to interfere when you're trying to concentrate on a child's feelings and situation. You'll be better equipped to deal with your own feelings at the same time you're dealing with children's feelings.

Getting caught off guard by strong feelings of your own may cause you to shift your focus from the children or frighten them with a response more intense than the situation warrants. This is why its important to review your personal history and put it into perspective before sharing with children. When you're prepared, you'll be able to handle your emotions and share them more appropriately. If you are aware of it, your emotional "spillover" is quite acceptable; it can help you be a positive role model.

How Do You Feel about Death?

The rest of this chapter offers a series of activities to help you become more comfortable with the personal and emotional aspects of death and loss. The activities are presented sequentially to allow you to investigate your history of death experiences by taking small steps. Try not to skip any activities. As you continue, keep in mind that the effort you apply to the activities will directly affect your ability to create the desired environment for children. Take a break now, if you feel the need. Find a pen and paper. Get comfortable physically. Then continue getting comfortable emotionally as you take steps to find out about yourself.

As you begin this study of your personal relationship with death and loss, remember the open environment concept. It is just as important for you to be open with yourself in these activities as it is for you to create an open environment for children. Let your memories and feelings come as they are—some painful, some fearful, some pleasant, some confusing. You may not always have an answer, or a feeling, or an idea. That's OK too.

Consider each concept seriously. If you are sincere and honest with yourself, the experience will be more helpful. Keep in mind that the way you respond may change over time. You may want to review these activities in the future to see how time and experience have affected you. Taking these first steps to self-awareness requires courage. Parents, caregivers, and teachers often avoid exploring their feelings regarding death and loss. Once you understand the full benefits for yourself and the children in your life, however, you will find the strength you need to explore your experiences and learn from them.

Activity: Finding Death in Daily Life

Death really is a part of our daily lives. Prove it to yourself by picking up your daily newspaper—any newspaper. Scan the headlines and stories. Notice the use of death-related words even when the story doesn't relate to death (for example, a boxing match that is "a killer," or the "deadly heat"). As you scan, keep a list of all the stories related to death and to loss. For example, you will find elements of loss in stories about businesses closing, athletic injuries, physical disabilities, car crashes, or rape.

Take Action

Stop now, review your newspaper, and make a list of stories with death-related words. Also list some of the terms here or on a another piece of paper. If you'd rather, simply use a marker and circle or highlight the death-related references you find.

_____

_____

_____

Consider These Questions

1. Did you have any trouble finding death- and loss-related stories or words? Why or why not?
2. Did any of the stories include references to feelings?
3. How do you feel after reading these stories? Why?
4. How did you feel about the use of death-related words in nondeath stories? Is it offensive? Acceptable? Why or why not?
5. How did you feel about the choices of coverage and emphasis regarding specific events?

Think about What You've Learned

You probably had no trouble finding death- and loss-related stories because they are a real part of our daily lives. Consider that the stories in the newspaper are only the ones an editor found noteworthy. In addition, they represent only one medium. Television, radio, literature, and the internet have similar degrees of death-related references.

If you have trouble finding death-related stories, it may be because you reviewed a small local newspaper. Check for related stories and obituaries in the weekend edition or a larger city newspaper.

Many stories tend to focus mainly on facts, a reflection of the reporter's objective style that we expect in a newspaper. If you had no emotional response to a story, the situation described was probably one where you were able to remain objective. But if a story included characters or events that reminded you of your family or friends, you probably had an emotional response. When a story hits closer to home, it's harder to remain objective.

Some stories use phrases like "I thought I'd die" or "dead tired." Such death-related phrases are common in the media and in our everyday conversation. Now that you've become aware of them, you'll probably notice them even more. Usually people aren't offended by these phrases. In fact, most people probably don't even think of them as related to death. The exception is when we have recently experienced a death or loss. When death touches us, all references to death in our society bring out more intense feelings.

You may also reflect upon events that have received significant coverage by media. You may realize that a majority of those media events involved the death of a well-respected or well-known person (for example John F. Kennedy, John Lennon, Princess Diana) or a major catastrophe, such as an earthquake, airline crash, bombing, or terrorist attack. Were these stories covered appropriately or were they sensationalized, exaggerated, dehumanized, or glorified? You might find some insight in exploring why your view may be different from the reporter's view.

Activity: Cultural Traditions and Religious or Spiritual Beliefs

The next step is to explore what your religious or spiritual beliefs and cultural traditions tell you about dealing with death and loss. Two activities are provided to guide your exploration. The first presents a series of statements for you to consider. Then you will decide whether you agree with, are undecided about, or disagree with the statements. In the second activity, you are asked to finish statements with whatever comes to mind. There are no right or wrong answers for either activity. You are simply recording and becoming aware of your opinions and beliefs.

We may be unable to identify our own cultural and religious beliefs because they are such an integral part of us or because they change as our life experiences change. It is important to take time to become aware of what they are at this time. The following activity will help you clarify some of your own beliefs, help you see how your beliefs may be different from others', and note how they influence your responses to death and loss.

Take Action—Step One

Read each statement and indicate whether you agree, are undecided, or disagree.

	Agree	Undecided	Disagree
1. Death occurs when the brain stops working.	☐	☐	☐
2. Funerals should be simple and dignified.	☐	☐	☐
3. Wakes should be celebrations of life.	☐	☐	☐
4. Children should not attend funerals	☐	☐	☐
5. Girls are more expressive than boys	☐	☐	☐
6. There is life after death.	☐	☐	☐
7. Embalming a dead body is necessary.	☐	☐	☐
8. It would be easier to handle death if it were sudden rather than after a prolonged illness.	☐	☐	☐
9. Cremation is not an acceptable practice.	☐	☐	☐
10. It is important that feelings associated with grief be expressed openly.	☐	☐	☐
11. The funeral should reflect the dead person's personality.	☐	☐	☐
12. I would rather die suddenly than after a prolonged illness.	☐	☐	☐
13. Euthanasia is a human right.	☐	☐	☐
14. Laughing around a grieving person is inconsiderate.	☐	☐	☐
15. Visiting hours at a funeral home are depressing.	☐	☐	☐
16. I would rather die at home than in a hospital.	☐	☐	☐
17. The funeral should reflect the dead person's religion.	☐	☐	☐
18. People who donate organs are denying the inevitability of death.	☐	☐	☐
19. I hope to outlive my life partner.	☐	☐	☐
20. Funerals are too expensive.	☐	☐	☐
21. Only cemeteries that have been blessed by religious leaders are acceptable.	☐	☐	☐
22. The dead person should be dressed completely in white.	☐	☐	☐
23. Flowers and music are important parts of memorial services.	☐	☐	☐
24. Anyone who is interested should be allowed to participate in the memorial service.	☐	☐	☐
25. Vaults are a necessary part of the burial.	☐	☐	☐

		Agree	Undecided	Disagree
26.	Relatives of the dead person must stay awake until the body is buried.	☐	☐	☐
27.	Funeral homes are not necessary.	☐	☐	☐
28.	Family and friends should not see the body actually being lowered into the grave.	☐	☐	☐
29.	A funeral oration should not be given over a person who has committed suicide.	☐	☐	☐
30.	Death-related rituals end when the body is lowered into the ground or the ashes are disposed of.	☐	☐	☐

Take Action—Step Two

Read the following sentence beginnings and finish the statement in your own words.

1. Religious rituals are important because

_____

_____

2. Funeral directors are

_____

_____

3. Life after death means

_____

_____

4. Memorial services should be planned and discussed before a death because

_____

_____

5. Behavior at a funeral should be

_____

_____

6. Cemeteries are

_____

_____

7. Cremated ashes should be

_____

_____

8. The most important factor in planning a funeral is

_____

_____

9. Visiting the family and friends is important because

_____

_____

10. A person is dead when

_____

_____

11. If I had a fatal illness, I'd want

_____

_____

Consider These Questions

1. Were your answers for both activities based on your religious or spiritual beliefs?
2. Were your answers based on your experience with death?
3. Which questions were the easiest to answer? Why do you think they were easy?
4. Which questions were most difficult to answer? Why do you think they were difficult?
5. Did you feel emotional about any statements with which you agreed? Disagreed? Why or why not?

Think about What You've Learned

From the Amish custom of dressing the dead body in white to the way crying girls are accepted while crying boys are not, cultural and religious or spiritual beliefs influence our lives. These beliefs are so ingrained in us that we often react to other people's ideas with disbelief or disgust. Did you feel that way at any point while completing the previous activities? Many people do.

There is no need to adopt someone else's beliefs as your own. There is a need, however, to accept others' beliefs as their own. An awareness of the great variety of traditions related to death will help you avoid negative responses to children's beliefs and questions. Your awareness is a major step toward creating the open environment children need.

Did you learn anything new about yourself through your answers? Did you learn anything new about the range of death-related beliefs and traditions? Were you surprised by some statements? Were some confusing? Did this pique your curiosity about others' views?

Activity: Your Experiences with Loss

Most parents, caregivers, and teachers don't believe they are adequately trained to teach about death and loss. Although you may not have any formal education in the field, this activity will prove that you do have experience with loss.

Take Action

Review this list of events or situations. Place a check mark beside the ones you have experienced at some time in your life.

Losses Related to Age	Losses Related to Everyday Living	Obvious Losses
☐ loss of childhood dreams	☐ loss of job	☐ separation
☐ loss of puppy love	☐ loss of money	☐ divorce
☐ loss of crushes	☐ moving	☐ end of a friendship
☐ leaving school	☐ change of school	☐ end of a relationship
☐ leaving home	☐ change of teachers	☐ death of a pet
☐ change of job	☐ loss of property	☐ death of grandparent
☐ loss of youth	☐ loss of confidence	☐ death of parent
☐ loss of virginity	☐ loss of security	☐ death of friend
☐ loss of health	☐ loss of a cherished ideal	☐ death of child
☐ menopause	☐ loss of a long-term goal	☐ death of partner
☐ retirement	☐ change of relationship	
☐ loss of physical functioning		
☐ loss of mental functioning		

Now review the list again. This time, pause briefly at each check mark to recall any feelings you experienced associated with the events. Write down how you felt, so you can examine your feelings again later.

Consider These Questions

1. Were you surprised by the number of experiences you checked?
2. Did the feelings come easily?
3. Think about the range of feelings you experienced. Were all your feelings in the "sad" category or were they varied?

Think about What You've Learned

Experience is a good teacher. It increases your range of knowledge, your awareness of what you do and don't know, and your understanding of the personal impact of experience. Most people are surprised by how much experience they have had with death and loss and how much they remember about their experiences. Why? Because they've probably spent a lot of time and energy trying to put those "bad" times and feelings behind them, getting on with their lives, and trying to forget. But people don't really forget. In fact, it's helpful to remember. Remembering and reflecting on those experiences and memories helps us learn and grow.

People often avoid memories because of the sadness involved. But you may be finding that not all your feelings were sad. You might not have allowed yourself to note feelings that weren't sad because you felt they were inappropriate. Feelings of relief, love, and pleasure are common and appropriate responses to memories of death- or loss-related experiences. The familiar phrase "Better to have loved and lost than never to have loved at all" sums up a big part of this concept. You may have been relieved that a person didn't have to suffer any longer or that

you didn't have to watch him or her suffer. You will find more about the range of feelings associated with death and loss in chapter 3, "Learning What Children Need to Know about Death."

What you feel is not as important as the fact that you do feel. Death and loss are natural parts of life. They are not small and meaningless. Quite the contrary—loss of a human relationship, regardless of the cause, deserves to be treated with respect. We can learn important lessons as our lives continue beyond the loss.

Activity: Personal Experiences with Death

The next two activities will examine your personal experiences with death and loss and use these experiences to expand your death education training. If you've been reading and thinking about this subject for a while, you may want to take a stretch break or a deep breath. Relax and prepare to let your experiences and your feelings move you to another level of understanding death as a natural part of life.

Take Action—Step One

Take some time to reflect on the following questions. Write down your answers so you can look back at them now and later. Try to remember your first experience with death or significant loss.

- Who died or what was lost?
- What was your relationship to the person or animal that died?
- When did the death or loss occur?
- How old were you at the time?
- Can you remember any of the feelings you had? What were they?
- What were other people doing during those first few days after the death or loss?
- Were you allowed to help with or participate in any of the activities?
- Did you have any questions? What were some of your questions?
- Did someone answer your questions?
- Did you receive any comforting? If yes, who comforted you? If yes, what did they do to comfort you? If not, what comfort would you have liked?

- If you could, would you change anything that happened?
- Do you still talk and reminisce about the person or animal that died or the events around the death or loss?

Take Action—Step Two

Try to remember a more recent experience with death or loss. Take time to reflect on the list of questions in step one. Write down your answers again so you can look back at them later.

Consider These Questions

Review and compare your answers to your two different experiences with death or loss.

- What similarities did you find between the two experiences?
- What differences did you find between the two experiences?
- Why do you think differences existed?
- What knowledge did you gain from these experiences?
- What impact did these events have on your attitude toward death and loss?
- If you wanted to change some of the circumstances:
  - Why do you think you wanted the changes?
  - How do you think the changes would have helped?
- What impact did others have on your experiences?
- Did you actually feel some of the same feelings while you were remembering?
- How do you feel when you or other people talk about the death or loss?
- What impact do you think your experiences will have or have had on children?

Think about What You've Learned

No two death experiences are the same. Each detail of the situation can influence your reaction. Your current feelings may be very different from your feelings at the time of the death or loss. Your own age and the age of the person who died have an impact on your experience, too. For example, it is common for the death of a seven-year-old and the death of a seventy-six-year-old to bring out different reactions among family and friends. Children understand death in different ways at different ages; therefore, their reactions and memories will be different as well.

Relationships also influence your experiences. Your closeness with the person who died affects your response. Your closeness to other family and friends also affects you. In your experiences, did adults keep busy with rituals and tell children not to worry? This situation is common. Adults often become so engrossed in their own grief and activities that they forget or never become aware that children feel sad too and may need meaningful activity to cope with death or loss.

Often people ask questions to try to find meaning in the situation. It's our uniquely human way of trying to get our minds to understand the loss. Children often are discouraged from questioning—sometimes adults are, too. Although the potential for harm is greater when children's questions are ignored, adults also can be hurt. You may have been made to feel that your questioning was morbid, nosy, or inconsiderate. In reality, questioning is the way you come to accept the death and learn from the loss experience.

Sometimes death and loss experiences lead us to make changes the next time. Death experiences make us aware that some things in life can be controlled and some cannot. You might realize that although you can't change the illness, accident, or death, you can take control of some of the events surrounding the death. You can decide how the funeral will take place, let yourself cry more, keep yourself busier, or ask for the comfort you need. Any action you take will balance, however slightly, your loss of control over death and loss.

When you thought about what would make you feel better, did you think about what comfort means to you? Did you think about how to comfort someone else? Comforting comes in many forms, but it usually involves interaction with other human beings. You also may need time alone, but not *only* time alone. People need to know that others understand the depth of their feelings. Sharing your feelings is a primary source of comfort. It can be fulfilled by friends, family, religion, spirituality, or any combination of these. Seek comfort in whatever ways make you feel stronger.

Some people seek comfort in memories of the one who died. They enjoy telling and hearing stories about him or her and about the events surrounding the death. If this comforts you, allow it to continue. You may think of it this way: When the person no longer exists in body, what do you have left? The memories. When the memories include a feeling of love, you may be struck by the awareness that the love still exists. If these stories seem too hurtful or fail to provide comfort, you can choose not to think of them. You have control of the memories. Do you want to embrace them or avoid them? Do you want to share them and let them comfort you? Memories can be powerful and often are helpful and pleasant. Remembering the past is healthy when it helps you live for the present and plan for the future.

As you remembered your experiences, some of your feelings and thoughts may have been unique, while others may have been common human responses. Some of your feelings and thoughts may have been painful and difficult, while others may have been pleasant. Still others may have been confusing and worrisome. The important lesson is to recognize your uniqueness even while knowing you are not alone in your reactions. Enjoy and build on positive feelings while respecting and learning from difficult ones. Leave your mind open for answers to confusing questions. Time and experience still may have lessons to offer.

Activity: Thinking about Your Own Death

This last step in the self-exploration process is the most personal activity. You will be asked to think about your own death. Each of the previous steps has prepared you for this last activity. You know how to balance yourself by looking at difficult feelings as lessons and using positive feelings for comfort. As you completed the other activities, you've probably made some mental notes already about things you liked and didn't like. Now is the time to give some order to those notes and plan your own memorial events.

Take Action

Think about whether or not you want a memorial service. Then, if you do, think about your own memorial service and burial rituals using the following statements. Select one of the answers given, or write your own answer for each blank.

1. I want a *big/small/*_____funeral.
2. I hope that people at my funeral are *happy/sad/*_____ .
3. I want music to be *quiet/religious/upbeat/*_____ .
4. I want the service to be *traditional/a unique reflection of me/*_____ _____ .
5. The service should be *religious/spiritual/nonreligious/*_____ .
6. The service should be *private/public/*_____ .
7. I want the service to be *directed by professionals/ include my family and friends/*_____ _____ _____ .
8. I want the decorations to be *colorful/extravagant/plain/simple/*_____ .
9. I want people to make memorials by giving *flowers/donations to family/donations to charity/*_____ _____ .
10. I would like to be *buried/cremated/*_____ .
11. If buried, I want an *airtight casket and vault/a simple wooden coffin/* _____ _____ .
12. If cremated, I want my ashes to be *kept in a mausoleum/buried/scattered/kept with my family/*_____ _____ .
13. Describe any other details about your memorial and the related rituals (for example, epitaph, tombstone, obituary, procession to cemetery, family involvement, how you want to be remembered, and so on).

_____

_____

_____

_____

_____

_____

_____

Consider These Questions

- How did you feel about making decisions and writing about your own death?
- Were some parts harder than others? If so, why?
- Did you surprise yourself with any answers?
- Did you describe a traditional or nontraditional service?
- How do you think your family and friends would react to your choices?
- Would you consider sharing this information with family? With friends?
- What other necessary decisions might be related to your own death? Do you want to donate organs? Who will make health care decisions for you if you are unable to make them?

Think about What You've Learned

Were you prepared for this step? Some people believe that you are never prepared to accept losses or your own death. Do you agree? Did this chapter help you see the value of exploring your beliefs and feelings? Whether you were able to complete this activity or not, don't try to compare yourself with anyone else. You've probably gone as far as you can for now.

The next time you review the chapter you may decide to explore further or change your current responses. You are in the process of exploring your life, death, and loss experiences and learning from them. Taking these steps toward self-awareness and acceptance of death as part of life often makes our lives fuller. How do you feel about this?

Did your responses surprise you? Why? Was it because you were able to handle the thought of your own death better than you thought you could? Was it because you are less traditional than you thought you were? Maybe you realized that your religion is more important to you than you thought. Or you realized that you aren't afraid of dying. Are you concerned about how your death will affect your family and friends? Have you made choices based on what you think your family would want?

If you're aware of being surprised, for whatever reasons, congratulate yourself on your honesty and on creating an open environment in which to explore your personal attitudes toward death. When you're ready, you may want to take time to share your experiences with friends and family. Even if they're not open to discussing death, you can let them know that you're considering these issues.

The Next Step

These activities have brought you through self-discovery in stages, introducing increasingly personal and emotional questions at each level. When you take small steps like this, you're able to handle bigger concepts. Your experience here can serve as a guide when you're working with children. As you implement the activities for children in this book, you'll notice that they are presented in small stages. As parents, caregivers, or teachers, you'll decide where to start and how fast and how far the children can go in their exploration of death and loss.

2
Understanding How Children Learn about Death

Stages of Understanding
Lessons from the Media
Lessons from Culture
Lessons from Society and Language
Lessons from Religion and Spirituality

Whether children are aware of it or not, death and loss are part of their lives. Children watch television, read or hear stories, watch adults grieve, overhear hushed voices, change homes, change parents, change schools, hear prayers, see funeral processions, step on spiders, lose a special teddy bear, and "die" over and over again in video games. In addition, children increasingly are made aware of death and loss directly through media coverage of school shootings, natural disasters, fatal accidents, political assassinations, war, and terrorism. In the case of school shootings, even when far away, they occur in the child's world. As a result, they may have a huge impact on the children's sense of safety as well as their understanding of death. Children's experiences may come from the media, from customs and language in their culture, from their religious or spiritual training, from actual death experiences, or from any combination of these things. Regardless of the source, messages are being sent, and children are receiving them.

Depending on the age of the child at the time of the experience, these messages will vary. The younger the child, the fuzzier the message, leaving room for different interpretations. The older the child, the clearer the message. Children learn about death in small steps as their experiences and their abilities to think expand. As a result, you may find that you will revisit a death or loss experience with children as they progress through stages of understanding. Your job is to discern what children in your life already know and what they are capable of learning at each stage. When you can do this, you'll be able to make the messages about death and loss clearer and more meaningful.

You needn't have all the answers. You just have to help children with their next steps. At some point, you may even be learning together. That's one of the joys of the safe and nurturing environment being promoted here. You have the freedom to say, "I don't know, but let's find out together."

Stages of Understanding

In general, young children understand the concrete or physical world first. As they get older, they learn to reason and think about things they can't see or touch. Growth in their abilities occurs in predictable stages well established by child psychologists, based on a child's readiness to understand new information. A child's readiness to move on depends on how fully the current stage is explored.

Understanding How Children Learn about Death

Children move through developmental stages at different rates depending on the intensity of their experiences, the amount of adult guidance they receive, and the innate abilities of each child. Because of these individual differences, specific ages associated with each stage are just reference points. The *sequence* of stages is what is important—not specific ages. The ages are included in this discussion only as general guides.

Children follow these predictable stages in developing their understanding of death and loss, just as they do with other subjects. When they first acknowledge death, they see it as *reversible, avoidable, and impersonal.* By the time they are nine or ten they are able to see death as *final, inevitable, and personal.* The following sections will define these terms and describe how children move through four typical developmental stages: under age three, ages three through five, ages six through eight, and ages nine and over.

Stage One: Under Age Three

Children in stage one have limited verbal abilities, which makes them a difficult group to study. As a result, there are varied opinions and little research to confirm what children understand at this stage. We can, however, make some logical assumptions.

Some research studies found that children under three do react to and understand some aspects of death. As a result, we must acknowledge that these responses are *possible.* Whether or not they are typical is less important.

Also, it is logical that if children have individual differences in ability, adult guidance, and degree of experience, then it would be possible for some two-year-olds to understand death and react to it. For example, an observant parent or teacher of a bright one- or two-year-old may notice a behavior change when something or someone important in the child's life is missing. Children's artwork may show indications of awareness or understanding as well. It seems clear that children don't need to understand death fully to react to it.

The fact that very young children don't use words the way older children and adults do does not mean they don't experience similar feelings of loss. Limited verbal ability may be the reason that these youngest children often are thought to have a limited understanding of death and loss. Whatever observations or assumptions you make, be careful not to extend the assumption of understanding to include all children under three years old.

Stage Two: Ages Three Through Five

Four developmental characteristics affect children's understanding of death during this stage: inability to perceive time, egocentrism, animism, and magical thinking.

At this stage, children have a limited concept of the first characteristic—*sense of time.* Although they may be learning about yesterday and tomorrow, anything longer than that is quite unreal to them. As a result, the child is unable to see death as final. Instead, death is commonly viewed as temporary. For example, "Grandma is dead today, but she'll be back another day."

A second characteristic of this stage is inability to see the world from someone else's perspective—*egocentrism.* Although egocentrism in adults indicates immaturity, in children it is a normal, acceptable stage of development. This stage allows children to completely disregard a death that doesn't come close enough to touch their world directly. It is not seen as personal. For example, children at this stage often surprise adults with what appears to be a matter-of-fact, calm acceptance of death. They may be accepting the words, but the words don't have any real meaning in their lives.

On the other hand, as a result of being egocentric, preschool children may believe that a death or loss is a result or consequence of their own actions. This response presents one of the greatest challenges for parents, caregivers, and teachers when talking to children about death. If any child expresses a sense of *responsibility* for a loss or for a natural or accidental death, he or she *must* be reassured that this is *not so.* This approach appears to contradict the earlier discussion about developing an open environment with an accepting attitude. The accepting attitude holds true for all other feelings children express. But accepting a child's feelings of responsibility for a death is clearly harmful and inappropriate. Such guilt may be held emotionally for years, causing great distress for the individual. Therefore, guilt and responsibility are exceptions to the rule of accepting *all* feelings.

Animism, the third characteristic of this stage, refers to the tendency to believe that inanimate objects, such as rocks and blankets, are alive. Preschool children may not make the distinction between animate and inanimate objects. Thus, they have difficulty understanding the physical difference between life and death. Death appears to be just a different state, like hungry or tired, not the absence of life. This perspective also accounts for some children's ability to respond calmly. They may not understand the full meaning of death that typically causes adult responses.

Understanding How Children Learn about Death

Finally, a child in stage two engages in *magical thinking*. Children believe that people and objects have power to make other people and objects do things. For example, children may conclude that if they never break another house rule, their divorced parents will get back together. Or if the child gives Granddad a lucky rabbit's foot, then Granddad won't die. A resourceful child will use this magical thinking to "fix it," or find a solution with a happy ending. Magical thinking is what allows a child to see death as reversible and avoidable.

Stage Three: Ages Six Through Eight

This period is a major *transitional stage* for children. Initially, they are learning to see death as final and then inevitable for all living things except themselves. By the end of this stage they also may understand that death is personal. Because there is such a drastic change of view during this stage, you will see greater differences between individual children—and even within one child as he or she matures from age six to eight.

Children experience great conflict as they learn the biological fact of death's inevitability yet still hold onto the magic of "not me." Their early views of death give way as they develop an understanding of the depth of loss. Although words we use to describe our adult view of death seem simple, for children to understand fully the concepts of final, inevitable, and personal, they must take some huge steps. The final step taken in developing the full adult view of death is understanding that death is personal.

During this third developmental stage, children are very interested in death, especially physical details. They will have a million questions for a concerned and available adult. They want to know about the causes of death, the biological details of the disease and dying process, rituals associated with death, and physical aspects like coffins, tombstones, and funeral homes. As these concepts become clearer, many children in this stage begin questioning what happens after death as they move into the next stage of development.

Although questioning at this stage may be relentless and even gruesome from our adult perspectives, it is critical that adults maintain an open environment. Children need to be free to ask anything. The key is to stay focused on the reason for their questions. They are simply attempting to master this aspect of their world. They are truly curious. Their emotions may be put on hold temporarily while they investigate these physical concepts. Avoid the temptation to impose adult interpretations on the questions. Simply answer them in the objective manner in which they are asked.

Stage Four: Ages Nine and Over

Somewhere around age nine or ten, most children reach an adultlike understanding of death. They understand that death is final, inevitable, and personal. They can define death in medical and biological terms and can think about death in an abstract manner. At this time, children can begin to grasp metaphors and similes often used in discussions and literature related to death. For example, people "live on in our memories" or are "given back to the earth to nurture new growth." This language often is pleasing and comforting to adults, but it can be confusing to children under the age of nine.

Although children in this stage may have the mental ability to understand the facts related to death, they might still be limited in their experiences with death and their ability to cope with the emotions involved. As you know, no one outgrows the need for emotional support at a time of death or loss.

Remember that the ages given here are just reference points for developmental stages. Factors other than age affect when a child will move into the next stage: a child's personal abilities, adult guidance, and the number and intensity of death- and loss-related experiences were mentioned earlier. Use these stages of understanding to help you "think like a child"—the tried and true way to improve your interactions.

The following sections provide details about the influences of media, culture, and religion. Regardless of the specific ages at which children develop death concepts, it is critical to understand that their concepts of death become increasingly more detailed, accurate, and factual over time.

Lessons from the Media

Children who watch television and movies, read books, and surf the internet are filing away important bits of information about death and loss. Although all these media sources include information about death, it is not their main purpose to teach about death. That's our job as parents, caregivers, and teachers. But children are learning from the media.

Media messages involving death are increasingly available and increasingly violent for children. When the spacecraft Challenger exploded in 1986, thousands of school children were watching. When the federal building in Oklahoma City was bombed, children were faced with the reality of children dying violently as the newscasters repeatedly focused their coverage on the day care deaths. News coverage of school shootings and terrorism continues to force children into an awareness of death as personal, whether or not they're old enough to understand this concept. In television shows, the proportion of violent deaths is greater than the proportion of violent deaths in real life. It is not balanced with examples of death as a natural part of life. So, children are seeing images that often are frightening, confusing, inconsistent, and unrealistic.

Unfortunately, these media messages may reinforce children's misconceptions. Parents, caregivers, and teachers must learn to work with media messages and help children interpret and clarify facts. To use media messages to help children develop a healthy understanding of death and loss, you must understand how media messages can affect them.

Television and Movies

Think about what children see on television. A news anchor calmly comments on the number of people killed in a war on the other side of the world. A reporter at the scene emotionally describes gruesome details of a fiery airline crash or a terrorist attack. A cartoon character gets flattened by a steamroller and, after a brief pause and a frown, gets up to continue a chase. A character in a weekly mystery series gets killed, only to show up the next week on a comedy show on another network. In movies, the dead person sometimes is portrayed as someone horrible who "deserved to die" or elderly and "ready to die."

Do you think a child might wonder why those people were killed or why the news anchor didn't seem to care about the dead people? Could children be frightened by details of a crash? Could they be interested in the details without any accompanying emotions? Using their imaginations, could children decide that the cartoon character got up because he was stronger than the steamroller or that the man who died on the mystery show got better because he wanted to be on the comedy show next week?

Do some people really deserve to die? Think about our language. If an elderly person can be "ready to die," is that what the high school basketball star meant when he said he was ready to die when his team lost the game? Are you confused? Think how confused children must be?

Now think about how children respond to these media images. Do they accept them? Do they ignore them? Do they worry about them? Do they fill in gaps in their understanding with their own imaginings? All of these responses are possible.

How do you know what your children are thinking? First, you need to know what they're watching. The best way to know what children are watching is to watch with them. Then, use the open environment you've created to help children understand their experiences. If they don't ask questions about what the story means, you can ask questions about what they're thinking or feeling. This is your chance to set the record straight. You can correct any inaccurate information and confusing misconceptions.

If you are a teacher you'll have less opportunity to watch television with children. But you can still ask questions about what they're watching and pay attention to what they're talking about to each other. As you begin a death education lesson, you can ask if they've seen any examples of your lesson concept on television. Was it in a movie or on the news—that is, was it fact or fiction? You can ask for facts, feelings, or other characters' responses, depending on your lesson focus. If an especially disturbing happening in your community is being shown or discussed on television, you can begin the next day at school with "How many of you heard about . . . ? What do you think about it?" Once again you can set the record straight, clarifying facts as necessary. Chapter 6, "Using Planned Learning Strategies and Children's Literature," includes an example of how to use media in teaching.

Literature

Children's literature also includes references to death that can have an influence on children's perceptions. Because books are a big part of many children's lives, adults need to know how to identify positive approaches in books and use children's literature appropriately. A child may choose a book with a negative approach, like depicting a grieving child being left alone with no adult comforter. You need to understand the impact this experience might have and discuss the child's fears. If you can allay the fears honestly, do that as well. For example, you might discuss why the child in the story was alone and why the child you're comforting won't have to worry about being alone.

When you're choosing a book, look for those with positive approaches. A positive presentation of death is defined in this book's introduction. Most children's books usually present only a small part of a death-related experience. Handling small steps at a time is a good way to deal with death education. Chapter 6 offers more help with using children's literature. An activity called "Feelings in Children's Stories" suggests ways to use literature. The last section of chapter 6 describes how to choose an appropriate book.

As you discuss the content of television, newspapers, radio, and literature that children are exposed to, you will have many opportunities to teach about death. We're not suggesting that you turn every activity into a structured learning experience. But understanding the influence of these materials and how to use them can help when you need to clarify or initiate a conversation about death or loss.

Lessons from Culture

In our culture, death and loss are thought of as significant human concerns. But all segments of our culture do not see them exactly the same way. For example, social and economic factors affect the time available for grief, money available for memorials, exposure to death and loss, and thus, overall attitudes about how to deal with death and loss. Broader cultural influences include our mobile society, video games, and indirect language that keeps death a taboo topic.

Time and Attention

We know that grieving for any death or loss takes time and attention. Some children learn that adults take time off work to make arrangements, deal with their feelings, share special time with family and friends, maybe even take a family vacation to ease the tensions. Others may learn that grief must be scheduled around work time—in the evenings and on weekends. Business and physical arrangements, such as finding a new home, enrolling children in new schools, or planning a funeral, may come first, with adult coping next, and children getting the limited time left over, if any. Time becomes a commodity, even a luxury, having a direct impact on the way children experience death and loss. Children who receive different amounts of time and attention may not respond in the same ways when coping with death and loss.

The Memorial Service

Children have a broad variety of experiences when attending a memorial service. Details of the memorial service may be affected by the amount of money available from family, friends, or other sources such as insurance. There are different grades of funeral homes to choose from, just as we have different grades of department stores for our shopping. If you use a funeral home, your choice determines the extravagance or simplicity of the physical setting and, sometimes, the amount of personal care you receive from the funeral director and staff. Although the core group of services offered by funeral homes is similar, there is great variety among funeral homes regarding the range of additional services such as limousines, hair styling, and burial options.

Many other choices you make depend on what you can afford. For example, sometimes evening hours for visitation or funerals are more expensive than daytime hours. If you request that memorial donations be sent to the family or to favorite charities or if friends and family have a low income level, there may be fewer flowers for decorations. These variations make children's experiences very different. As a result, their picture or perception of what is "right" or "normal" also may vary.

Another issue where people experience great differences of opinion is in the choice of an open or closed casket. An individual's culture and expectations will draw one person to choose an open casket, which would alienate another person.

Variations in Personal Experience

The degree of exposure to death and loss also creates varied experiences and responses for children in different social and economic groups. Some children may have to move into new homes, adjust to leaving old friends and making new ones, or even adjust to new parents or caregivers. Some might experience gang wars and violent, meaningless deaths.

At the other extreme are children who live in one neighborhood with few home changes and keep the same friends and parents through the years. They might experience only news reports of deaths of strangers and natural deaths of aging or seriously ill pets and loved ones.

Such extreme variations in experience have a profound effect on a child's understanding of death. When children change homes frequently, they may learn to be adaptable. When they have difficulty isolating a day when violence and loss are not involved, they may learn to ignore death or pretend it isn't real. They may wear themselves down fighting for change or trying to make sense of the experiences, or they may become angry and violent.

Lessons learned when children's home lives are stable, supportive, and non-violent are quite different. Children are able to confront difficulties in their lives, explore them freely, and learn from them. These positive experiences help children balance painful experiences related to death and loss. Such children are capable of seeing death and loss as a natural part of life.

Children also receive messages from their community. The ethnic background of their neighbors and their geographic location produce different views of life and death. A child from an urban area where cemeteries are crowded and surrounded closely with other buildings would have a very different idea of burial than a child from a rural area where cemeteries are sprawled in open country. A child who grows up observing loud, joyful wakes will have a different expectation than a child who observes a typically somber visitation.

Cultural messages are not as obvious as media messages, although their influences may be as strong or stronger. When a child's culture is the same as your own, it is difficult to be objective enough to identify the messages. Our culture is so much a part of us that separating ourselves from it is a challenge. But we need to try. Think about some death-related customs of your culture and the language you use to describe death and loss.

Some people believe in putting a death behind them as quickly and quietly as possible, while others believe that open mourning is helpful. Individuals from these two backgrounds will find it difficult to understand the other perspective. The quiet person may feel that being asked about the deceased is impolite because it's a personal matter. In contrast, the open person may feel that the quiet person is unfeeling if the death is not discussed.

The quiet, extremely private individual may be uncomfortable discussing funeral details or the death and end up saying things like "I was sorry to hear about your mother's passing. I hope all the arrangements worked out all right."

If this is how you would talk, it probably seems perfectly acceptable. But some people might respond with thoughts or words like "Why can't you ask me about the casket I picked out?" or "She didn't 'pass' anything—she died, and I miss her."

Lessons from Society and Language

Some of the lessons children learn about death and loss are the same throughout most social and economic groups. Some of these broad influences on children's perceptions are our mobile society, a depersonalization of death, and an unwillingness to speak about death directly. While all three aspects of our culture play a part in developing a child's view, the way we hide death with indirect language is the most critical. Fortunately, it is also the area where caring adults can make the most difference.

Our Mobile Society

The mobile society and depersonalization of death have overlapping influences on children. Because people move around so much, many children must get used to learning new school rules, making new friends, and saying goodbye to what's familiar. While this might improve adaptability of some children, for others, it might create a barrier to developing meaningful relationships.

In addition, our mobile society causes children to be more isolated from older generations of their families and thus, more isolated from natural deaths of those generations. Such isolation means that when children experience death, it is more likely to be in a hospital or on television than in their homes. As a result, death may seem less personal.

Video Games

Another example of depersonalization comes from an activity that almost all children experience—video games. When a video game is over, children often say, "I died." The object of many video games is to "kill" other characters or objects on the screen. Having more than one life for your character or earning additional lives throughout the course of the game is common. Based on the earlier discussion of children's stages in understanding, you can see how the video game experience might feed into the inability to distinguish between animate and inanimate objects.

Along with some cartoons, comic strips, and movies, video games can foster a child's belief that death is temporary. Even in the advanced stage of understanding, video games are likely to create a depersonalization or desensitization toward death. Being aware of these possibilities can help you see when a child needs your help in making distinctions between real death and the language used in video games.

Indirect Language

The way adults make references or avoid making references to death and loss also influences development of the child's view. Avoiding discussions about death and loss perpetuates the taboo and keeps the child uninformed. When adults use symbolic or indirect language to talk about death, they may be giving a child misleading or confusing information. Thus, unnecessary fears may be aroused in the child.

Consider the perspective of young children in the following examples: A child develops the flu two days after being told that a close relative died because he was "sick." A second child is told that a deceased grandparent "went away" months or even years earlier. Could this child be angry about being left without a goodbye? What if the parent has to "go away" on a business trip?

Another child is told that someone who died is "asleep" or "on a journey." What response would be expected from this child at bedtime or vacation time? Even if well-intended, indirect or symbolic language can send harmful messages.

The positive side is that adults *can learn* to speak openly and directly with children about death. Chapters 3 and 4 offer more suggestions for eliminating indirect language from your conversations with children about death.

Lessons from Religion and Spirituality

Unlike the varied and unplanned messages from media and culture, messages from religion and spirituality are presented with the purpose of teaching specific beliefs and values. Many religious and spiritual groups require certain beliefs and rituals related to death. This section discusses some examples of the different ways religious and spiritual groups approach life after death, funeral and memorial services, and burial and mourning rituals.

Most religions or spiritual groups have a common belief in life after death. Differences are found in various definitions of this life after death. For some, life after death means that the spirit or soul lives on in heaven, hell, or purgatory. Others believe in reincarnation, where the spirit or soul is physically reborn in another life form. Still others believe that the spirit lives on in human interactions, or memories, of surviving loved ones. Finally, some people believe that the spirit lives on in the earth as part of the natural cycle of decomposed matter nourishing new life.

Most religions and spiritual groups have a common belief that some type of memorial service is an important part of mourning the death of a loved one. Details of services can vary. In some religions or spiritual groups, the funeral service must be directed by a leader of the church. Other religions encourage, and some require, that those close to the one who has died participate in the service. Many churches are unconcerned about the specific location of the service. Some do not allow involvement of a funeral home.

Some religions and spiritual beliefs require a somber attitude, without music or flowers. Many religions have no rules about decoration. It may be commonly accepted that the more flowers the greater the tribute to the deceased. When the organizational teachings don't specify the behavior expected, however, you might see anything from a quiet, somber service to a loud celebration.

For some religions and spiritual beliefs, no differences occur in the funeral when suicide is the cause of death. Other religions have strict rules against a formal religious funeral for a person who has committed suicide.

The most commonly accepted way of dealing with the dead body is burial. Cremation is another alternative accepted by many religions, not accepted by some religions, and preferred by a few. When burial is chosen, some religions require that the cemetery be one that has been blessed by a church dignitary. Most religions allow individual choice regarding whether burial is in the ground or in a mausoleum.

Viewing the dead body is often a matter of choice. In some religions and spiritual groups, it is allowed only for the family. A few religions expect that family members will clean and care for the dead body. Some religions require that the body be dressed in all white. Some require that family members stay awake from the time of death until the time of burial. Some require that the casket be closed.

Children learn facts and attitudes as they develop their understanding of death. Facts are learned in stages as their minds expand and they are able to think in new ways. Regardless of their mental abilities, children are taking in messages at all ages from media, culture, and religion or spirituality. The amount of death-related experiences and adult guidance influences how children understand messages and how quickly they move through the stages toward an adult understanding of death.

Because children see different social and cultural pictures based on their individual experiences with death, their perceptions of what is "right" or "normal" are very different. In most cases, they are adopting attitudes of adults in their lives who are continuing a particular cultural perspective.

Although changes occur in cultural perspectives, for a new view to become accepted takes a long time. While death is still a taboo topic for many adults, children in your lives will be experiencing a change in cultural perspective when you help them to see death and loss as natural parts of life—important parts of life that can be shared growing experiences.

3
Learning What Children Need to Know about Death

Teaching Facts
Sharing Feelings
Sharing Beliefs
Teaching Coping Skills

Two general approaches can be used for teaching children about death and loss. Sometimes children may introduce the topic, at home or at school, as a result of something they saw on television, something they heard about, or a current death or loss experience. Or the topic of death and loss may be introduced through a planned series of learning strategies. Planned death education and activities to explore current death and loss experiences are both critical for a well-rounded, healthy learning experience.

Whichever approach you're using, four specific topic areas need to be considered—not all at once but in individual steps. You'll determine which topic area or combination of areas is most relevant and important for a specific situation. All four areas have to be covered eventually. All steps need to be taken so that children are able to understand the concepts and cope with their feelings, based on the developmental stages discussed in chapter 2.

This chapter provides background information to help you understand the four topic areas:

- teaching facts,
- sharing feelings,
- sharing beliefs, and
- teaching coping skills.

Teaching Facts

Learning facts is one step children need to take in their quest to understand death and loss in their lives. What do they need to know about death and loss? How do we, as concerned yet uncertain adults, approach the subject when guidelines from experts aren't clear-cut? How do we explain difficult concepts without causing fear, emotional pain, confusion, or mistrust? Although many of the answers to these questions depend on a child's readiness to understand facts, the following guidelines can be applied more generally.

Identify the Level of Understanding

First, look for clues that will identify children's level of understanding (as described in chapter 2). Accumulated history and current daily experiences tell much about children. Did the children see a funeral procession when they were riding the bus home from school yesterday? Did they see a gruesome murder being discussed on the evening news? How are they reacting? How do they describe the event? What questions do they ask?

If they announce the event with little emotion and quickly go on to the next activity, they may be in the stage typical of ages three through five. If they describe great detail and ask questions about physical aspects, they may be in the stage typical of ages six through eight. If they contemplate what their own funeral procession might look like, they are probably in the stage that is typical of ages nine and over.

If you pay attention to the language they use, you can find clues to children's level of understanding and the meaning of their words. When possible, use these same words to clarify terms and concepts.

Once you've identified the level of understanding, you can move on to the specific facts you want to teach. Facts don't change for different children. The amount of information, the degree of detail, and the language used, however, will vary with the developmental stage of children.

Tell the Truth

Adults know that half-truths and incorrect information lead to fear, misunderstanding, and mistrust. Think about someone who has lied to you. Did you trust the person after that? Probably not. The same thing is true of children. If you lie to them about death, they will be less trusting of you in the future.

For children, lack of trust in significant adults in their lives has serious consequences. If children realize that they can't trust information you're giving them about death and loss, they are likely to conclude that they can't trust *any* information you give them. (Maybe it's *not* really important to look both ways before you cross the street. Or maybe Grandpa didn't really love me.) Thus, distrust has the potential to cause harm or affect our memories or our feelings.

Children deserve to know the truth. As their interpreter, you have to decide how much they're able to cope with and understand. Resist the urge to use these limits to justify shielding children from reality. Respect the strength of their emotions and their ability to understand. Then give them direct, honest answers at the highest level you believe they will understand.

As you strive to determine what children are able to accept and understand, these questions might help:

- What do I see as the real question from the child's point of view?
- How much information and what degree of detail should be presented?
- How can I present information in a matter-of-fact, objective manner?

Think Like a Child

When reacting to children's questions and comments based on their own interpretation, adults may jump to conclusions far beyond a child's understanding. If a five-year-old asks, "What happens when a person dies?" the child may simply want to know that the body is taken to a funeral home where it is put in a casket to be buried. If an adult begins a discussion of heaven and hell, children may jump to frightening conclusions. For example, how easily a child might think, "Since I don't know how to fly to heaven, I will have to go to that bad place—hell." To avoid this unnecessary trauma and fear, remember the developmental abilities of children at different stages. Try to look at things from their point of view.

> Remember, there are no "right" answers. No one knows exactly what to say or when to say it. Trust your heart, your intuition, and your relationship with the children.

This responsibility may seem daunting. What if you don't give the right answers, aimed at the proper level of understanding? What if your answer is too long or too involved? These fears are natural. Trust your skills as parent, caregiver, or teacher. You've probably been communicating with children for years. You know that any time you discuss something, you follow up by looking for clues telling you the children understood. Use those same skills and clues when talking about death and loss.

Ask questions. Observe expressions and behavior. Know that some children will continue to ask questions until they feel confident in their understanding. If they don't, you can ask *them* questions. Their questions and their answers to your questions will help you decide whether they have understood your message. If they withdraw or act out, consider whether your message has prompted this behavior. Then, be prepared to clarify. Remember, there are no "right" answers. No one knows exactly what to say or when to say it. Trust your heart, your intuition, and your relationship with the children.

Let children lead the conversation as much as possible. If they're asking a specific question, they're probably ready to hear the answer. If they're repeating something heard on television, they may not be ready, but they need to begin a discussion anyway. If they stop asking questions, they've probably taken in as much as they can at the moment. If they continue asking questions, they still need and want to know more. Letting the children lead is also a good way to help you avoid unnecessary trauma. The overall guiding rule is that *everything said* must be the truth, but you don't have to *tell everything*. For example, we may decide to tell a child that a teacher died of AIDS, yet we have no need to describe the details of the symptoms and pain involved in the death—unless the children ask.

Avoid Judgment

Although there are no "right" answers, there *is* a right attitude. When talking to children about death and loss, it's important to avoid judgment. It's important to be matter-of-fact and objective when you present the facts. *Objective* doesn't mean "without feeling." Someone who is objective simply states facts without conveying approval or disapproval.

Having the right attitude extends even to what might be considered a concrete concept—biological death. Does death occur when the brain stops, when the heart stops, when the lungs stop, or when all three stop? There is no universally "right" answer; it depends on your beliefs. But acknowledging that all these views exist is the right *attitude,* that of nonjudgment.

When we move into the more subjective aspects of rituals, feelings, and beliefs, presenting the range of ideas is more important than judging which is appropriate. Parents and caregivers are free to let children know what they themselves believe. Teachers, however, need to emphasize that individual variations exist and are determined by individual beliefs and values. Right or wrong, approval or judgment, should not be part of the lesson.

Use Appropriate Language

Along with appropriate facts and attitude, consider appropriate language. (Refer to the table in chapter 4 for suggestions on using direct, meaningful language.) Remember that when you try to shield a child from painful details surrounding death and loss by substituting less direct words, you may unwittingly create fear or confusion. If death is being "asleep," then who would want to sleep? If death is a "trip to heaven," then "Why can't I go, too?" Once you become more comfortable discussing death and loss, you'll be able to resist the urge to use these euphemisms.

When you're working with younger children, resist using metaphors, too. Metaphors are too abstract for young children to understand. In an attempt to make sense of your metaphor, they may put the message into their own concrete terms. If a buried pet is said to be nourishment for flowers that will grow in the spring, a child's interpretation might be that the pet comes back to life and waters the plants or that the buried pet magically changes form and becomes a flower. Children given metaphors may end up with confusing thoughts that are difficult to overcome as they continue their climb to higher levels of understanding.

Sharing Feelings

As parents, caregivers, and teachers, we must approach helping children explore feelings by developing a thorough respect for each child's reactions and emotions. Focus on the fact that children *do* experience loss and grief. Believe that their feelings are as strong to them as ours are to us. This respect and compassion for children's views of life is the foundation of an ability to acknowledge, explore, accept, and discuss children's feelings.

If you don't know about acknowledging, here's how it works. A child says, "I'm so sad!" or withdraws from an activity normally considered fun and interesting. Adults often respond by trying to "make it all better" or even by ignoring the child's feeling for fear of handling it poorly or getting too involved. Some adults may not even recognize the sadness.

The thing to do is to *acknowledge the child's feelings*. You can say, "I can see (or hear) how sad you are. I get sad, too. It's OK to be sad." Then depending on the child and the situation, you can begin a discussion of related questions: "Why do you (we) feel sad? What do you (we) do when you (we) feel sad? What makes you (us) feel better when you're (we're) sad?"

When you ignore or "take over" a child's feelings, you reduce the child's power to handle feelings. The unspoken message is that "you can't handle this bad feeling, so I'll handle it for you." Your intentions may be good, but children need the chance to practice and express their feelings. With especially strong feelings like those associated with loss and grief, practice doesn't make perfect, either. But practice does help us learn important life lessons—"Life does go on," "I can handle this," "It won't last forever," and other attitudes that help people cope with difficult situations.

When you ignore a child's feelings, you lower the child's self-esteem. Not acknowledging feelings sends a message that children interpret in different— mostly harmful—ways. A child might conclude: "What I feel isn't important enough to comment about." Or "What I feel is wrong." Or "What I feel is so scary that even the grownups don't want to think about it." These messages arouse feelings that can be more confusing, painful, and frightening than the initial response to death and loss.

By acknowledging the child's feelings, you send these messages: "Your feelings are important. Your feelings are OK. Your feelings can be handled." And "You're important to me." Given these supportive messages, children are empowered to explore their feelings. Remember, we can't learn to cope with feelings until we have fully explored them. To learn from feelings, we have to experience them.

Once children's feelings are acknowledged, children and adults are free to explore them together. Sharing feelings with adults helps children practice expressing their own feelings. When children (and adults) learn to put their feelings into words and actions, a new area of support is opened. Children learn they can ask for help and support and receive it.

Sometimes just the act of sharing feelings spreads the weight of sadness between a child and adult. Don't you feel better when you know someone else knows and cares about how you feel? When children feel this kind of support and understanding, they are able to get through the immediate situation and break through to the other side. They remember the good feelings in their lives also. Then comes the awakening that they really can bear difficult problems and feelings in their lives. They realize that painful feelings don't last forever and life does go on.

Create an Open Environment

An open environment is particularly important. To help children explore feelings related to death and loss, create an environment where children's feelings are welcomed and accepted, where both adult and child feelings are discussed openly, and where children are comforted.

Remember, as discussed in chapter 1, you must be accepting and comfortable with your own feelings before you can provide the safe, caring, and nurturing environment children need. If you evaluate or judge children's feelings, you are putting children in a no-win situation. If they disagree with you, they may feel guilty or conclude that their own feelings are wrong—maybe even bad. And if they agree with you, they may be relieved at first, then begin to worry about whether their feelings will be "right" the next time.

Frequently, adults try to interpret children's words and meanings. Although adults assist children by helping to interpret events in their lives, it is important not to interpret their feelings. Simply accepting children's feelings at face value is enough. There are no "right" ways for adults to feel when grieving. There are no "right" ways for children to feel when grieving. In fact, some children may experience joy or relief when a death occurs. If so, it is usually a direct result of something in the relationship between the deceased and the surviving child. For example, a surviving sister may be happy when a terminally ill sibling dies because she no longer has to share her room. Such a response may feel uncomfortable or seem inappropriate to us as adults, but is possibly a very normal response from a child. If allowed to experience these emotions, children gradually will work through a range of other emotions, including those we may feel are more appropriate, like sadness or anger.

Learning What Children Need to Know about Death

There is one exception to this rule of accepting *all* feelings. When children express any sense of responsibility for a natural death or loss, they must be reassured, "It's not your fault!" A direct approach is crucial to making sure the child hears clearly that the death is not a result of something the child did or didn't do. A follow-up with an explanation of why or how the person died would be useful. Whether a child can understand the details or not, you are giving them the absolute truth and laying groundwork for further understanding at a later stage. In fact, this issue almost certainly will require repeated conversations and reassurances during the initial grieving and later as a child develops the ability for greater understanding.

Sharing your feelings with children is almost as important as encouraging them to share their feelings with you. While their feelings remain the focus of your sharing, telling them how you feel may open up new ideas or help them accept their own feelings more readily. If someone they admire—like you—feels differently, it gives them some new ways to look at things (when they're able).

> There is one exception to this rule of accepting *all* feelings. When children express any sense of responsibility for a natural death or loss, they must be reassured, "It's not your fault!"

Act as a Role Model

A death or loss experience is an important opportunity to role model for children. They can watch you express feelings, agree with feelings, or disagree with but respect feelings of others. Think about it: Did you have a role model for these feelings as a child? If you did, do you think the role model made it easier for you to learn to express yourself? If you didn't, when or how did you learn the language of feelings and how to express them?

So far, we've discussed words as the primary way of communicating support, acceptance, and encouragement. While words truly are powerful comforters, there are times when touch can be even more powerful. Degree and type of touch depends on the relationship between you and the child.

Obviously, parents and caregivers will be more physically involved with their children than teachers. Current social rules require great caution regarding touching children. But there may be times, at home or at school, when physical comfort is needed. A touch, a hug, or a knowing smile can have a profound effect on children. When you know a child is troubled or upset but you can't put the feelings into words, a touch can communicate your compassion. We all know that a picture is worth a thousand words. When dealing with death and loss, sometimes a touch can be worth a thousand words as well.

Sharing Beliefs

Sharing beliefs is another important area for parents, caregivers, and teachers to include in their death education plans. Sharing beliefs about death and loss is much like sharing feelings. A great range of different beliefs needs to be acknowledged, respected, explored, accepted, and discussed. Some are based in religion or spirituality, while others come from socially accepted practices or norms. How do you deal with diversity and still provide lessons that children can understand?

The same basic guidelines also work here. You share yourself and your viewpoints. You maintain an open, welcome environment. You resist the urge to shield children from painful parts of life.

Different Roles of Parents, Caregivers, and Teachers

Sharing beliefs is an area where parents, caregivers, and teachers may find the greatest differences among their roles. Feelings and facts are almost universal, and acceptance of other viewpoints in these areas is not usually threatening or distasteful. With personal beliefs, however, parents and caregivers may focus on presenting specific beliefs of their family and their religion or spirituality group. Teachers must present a variety of beliefs held within the school, community, country, or world without endorsing any particular belief.

Teachers usually would not choose to present only one personal or religious or spiritual view. Teachers have a responsibility to represent a balanced view, one showing a range of different beliefs. If a teacher is not objective in this area, students may be confused or angry because their own cultures are not recognized in the classroom.

In contrast, parents or caregivers explain their personal religious, spiritual, and cultural beliefs to their children. Parents or caregivers might adopt a teacher's focus by presenting a variety of beliefs and urging their children to accept others' beliefs even when they disagree. They are likely to end, however, by encouraging their children to adopt beliefs similar to their own. When children are allowed to choose their own beliefs, parents and caregivers need to share many possibilities with them so that they can understand the choices.

Small Steps, Open Environment

A child's beliefs need to be explored in small steps—and in an open, caring, and supportive environment. When you make death and loss a natural, comfortable topic in your home or classroom, you are showing that loss is a part of life. If you whisper or fidget nervously when children bring up the subject, they will sense that you are uncomfortable discussing death and loss and may stop asking questions.

When you are natural in your voice and mannerisms, children will know that it's OK to ask "What is heaven?" and "Why did the minister say Uncle Joe had gone to a better place?" They will feel free to express their theories as this seven-year-old child did. "I think when a person dies their body is gone except for their brain. I think their brain goes into another person's brain and then the living person knows everything that the dead person knew. That's why some people are smarter than others."

Just as with denying children's feelings, denying their beliefs reduces their self-esteem and limits their opportunity to practice expressing and getting feedback on their thoughts—clearly obstacles to growing and developing positively. Allowing children to explore and express their beliefs and learn from their exploration tells them they can come to you with their ideas. Then, you are given the opportunity to clarify or simply acknowledge their concepts as needed.

Acknowledge the Importance of Death and Loss

When adults attempt to shield children from difficult situations and feelings in life, they often cause children to believe that these situations are unimportant, children may believe related feelings are unimportant, and worst of all, that children themselves are unimportant.

Death and loss *are* important parts of life. When a big brother goes away to college or simply doesn't spend time with a little brother anymore, the little brother may experience a severe loss. When someone we love moves away or dies, we don't want children to believe that it's not important enough to discuss. We don't want them to think that if they move away or die, we won't miss them.

Relationships with friends and loved ones are crucial to our well-being. Loss of these relationships through whatever means affects us greatly. We need to acknowledge and experience all the feelings associated with loss. We can feel bad, even get mad, and learn how to move beyond difficult times and become stronger individuals. Our experiences of grief and loss develop beliefs that help us cope with life experiences.

Teaching Coping Skills

The fourth area of death and loss education is teaching coping skills. Remember two key elements when providing guidance in this area: involvement and memories. These are the same coping mechanisms adults find helpful. Because children may experience similar feelings of grief, they also may benefit from these elements that provide comfort and allow them to cope.

Involve Children in Activities

Being involved means taking actions related to death or loss. Most adults and children feel a sense of helplessness when a death or loss occurs. This feeling is natural since in most circumstances, we can't do anything to replace the loss or keep our loved one from dying. Such a loss of control and hope often is associated with depression. To some degree, taking action can help individuals keep control and maintain hope in their lives.

When children move and change schools, they need to take action. For example, making new friends and learning new rules gives them a positive focus during a difficult time. When they succeed, their self-esteem is increased.

Similarly, when children know someone who has died, they need to be involved in related activities. Adults can provide positive role models for children at this time by including them in many of the activities. Children can help cook, deliver food, make cards, choose flowers, make a memorial notebook, and even help chose a gravestone. Being involved provides a focus. Helping others makes children feel good about themselves.

Once again, think about a child's level of understanding before you decide what activities to offer. Do not force children to participate in these activities. Always offer them the *opportunity* to participate. Many children will want to. They like to imitate their parents and teachers. They want to feel a part of things.

Tell children what you plan to do, why you do it, and possibly how it makes you feel. Then, if they want to, let children know how they can help. Most children will be either flattered to be asked or curious enough to take action. It's also OK if they're not interested. When they are ready, they will accept your offer.

What about the funeral itself? Should children be involved in the funeral? It depends. Consider questions such as these: What type of service will it be? Will adults be available to support children during the service? If the funeral is to be a long, formal, religious ceremony, it might not be realistic to expect a young child to sit through it. If the ceremony involves participation by the guests and has the feel of celebration, it might be a problem for a child who is quiet, angry, or traumatized by the death. But other children might feel comfortable in the same situation.

Use your knowledge of the child and your intuition to decide whether the specific circumstances are ones that the child can handle. Before you encourage children to attend the funeral, make sure that an adult will be available to provide support during the service. Funerals can arouse unexpected feelings in both adults and children. An adult should be standing by in case a child needs help.

When the conditions and support are appropriate and a child does attend funeral services, it can be a powerful teaching tool. Children will have opportunities to watch how adults comfort each other, comfort themselves, and grieve. Children can see and learn a variety of responses and experience their own feelings in the situations. No planned learning strategies you might provide for children can be as influential as these real experiences. Planned activities, however, still have an important role in children's development. They help prepare children for when real death occurs.

Use Memories for Comfort

Adults may put memories on hold and bring them out when they can cope with them. Children need their memories kept close at hand. Memories of the love and comfort they received from the person who died are especially helpful. Often, by remembering the love and comfort, children are able to still feel loved and comforted. It's reassuring to know that these feelings don't disappear when loved ones die.

As children share and experience their memories, you'll observe that they may have a short attention span. Although they need to continue to work with their memories over a period of many weeks, months, or years, they will do so in brief moments. They may initiate numerous conversations each day related to their memories of a loss, yet each conversation may only last for a few minutes. You also may notice different attitudes from day to day. Although children need to explore memories over time, they also need to take breaks to deal with their limited attention span.

Even hurtful memories can be important to children. If their grief for the deceased includes unpleasant feelings, the memories are still important. Because children tend to fill gaps in information with their own imaginative ideas, children often are much more frightened by a lack of memories. Their imagined details or their egocentric thinking may cause fear, confusion, and guilt.

If no one talks about Uncle Joe, possibly because he was an unpleasant person to be around, children might conclude that if they themselves are not "good," no one will remember them. They may not be able to verbalize such a feeling. It may be only an uncomfortable feeling somewhere in the subconscious. But the underlying attitude they will have learned is that life and death are insignificant.

On the other hand, acknowledging memories acknowledges the importance of losses. Learning to use memories for comfort is a step toward successfully handling feelings of loss. Just as mastery of math concepts builds self-esteem, mastery of difficult feelings can build self-esteem.

Keeping memories alive also helps children acknowledge that the dead person or pet or other lost thing was an important part of their lives and allows them to let go of the loss gradually. Memories can fill some of the empty spaces left when a death or loss occurs. As time goes by, memories may be needed less frequently. Remembering will always be an important way of coping with death and loss.

4
Answering Children's Questions

Guidelines for Discussing Death and Loss with Children
Examples of Questions and Responses

This chapter offers guidelines for discussing death and loss with children and provides suggestions for answering some specific questions they might ask. You also will find a chart to help you replace potentially harmful indirect or symbolic language with direct language that helps to build understanding.

Guidelines for Discussing Death and Loss with Children

When talking to younger children, use concrete terms and short answers. You often will find yourself giving information in response to facial expressions or behavior instead of direct questions. Young children may be unable to put their questions into feelings or words. Look to their actions for clues. Often your tone of voice and the physical comfort you can offer will be more important than the exact words you use.

For older children, give answers that leave room for their concepts to grow. It's OK to use some words they might not know if you're in a situation where they can ask questions to clarify. Try to find out what brought the question to the child's mind. The reason for asking can help you decide how much detail to give. As you continue to answer children's questions throughout their developmental stages, they'll understand more and more of what you're saying.

Make sure you know what children are really asking. Ask questions to clarify what you have heard. As always, answer in an open environment with familiar expressions of comfort you usually use (based on your relationship)—touches, hugs, smiles, a loving tone of voice. As you ask questions, children will guide you with their answers. This concept is like the story about the young child who asked where babies come from. After the parent's detailed discussion about procreation, the child replied that his friend came from the local hospital. Apparently the child just wanted to know the hospital where he was born. If you are uncertain about how much detail to give, follow the child's lead. A general rule is that if a child can form a question he or she can cope with the response. Also, if children keep asking questions they need to know more. When they stop asking questions they have as much as they can process at the time.

Balance emotions with matter-of-factness. Even though death is a difficult topic, we can still talk about it and try to understand and feel better together. Take some

Answering Children's Questions

time for yourself. If you feel overly emotional, choose another time for your discussion with the children—when you're more able to think about their needs. For children to be able to hear the whole message, a degree of control is needed. If you're too emotional, they can't understand the words. On the other hand, if you show no emotion, the words may seem too harsh or be confusing. Finding a balance, however difficult, increases the ability of children to hear and understand the messages.

When children ask a question about feelings, focus on emotional answers and support. When their questions are factual, focus on informative answers. Even if what they ask surprises you, try to accept it as important and give the thoughtful answers children's questions deserve.

Be honest, truthful, and caring. Regardless of the type of question or developmental stage of the child, your answers should be honest, truthful, and caring. After listening carefully to a child's questions or comments, decide whether you should give explanations, provide comfort, or ask more questions to be sure you understand the question. Try not to worry about having the right answers; if you speak honestly and from your heart, your answer will be meaningful. Sincerity can make up for any awkwardness, and it leaves the door open for further questions as needed.

Questions or comments that reveal a child's feeling of responsibility for the death are the *only* ones that should *not* be accepted. When this occurs, you must be very direct and forceful—making sure the child understands that he or she is not to blame. Repeat the message as often as necessary until you're sure it is understood and that the real cause (if known) is accepted by the child. This reassurance may take days, weeks, or years. Continue until you're sure the child fully understands.

Although children need to learn both facts and emotional coping skills related to death, they may be able to concentrate on only one aspect at a time. Over time, you'll be able to touch on all the important elements of teaching children about death and loss. Remember, all children are aware of death and loss at some level. They may be too young to put their questions into words. They may be old enough but too quiet or shy. But they are aware of and thinking about the death-related experiences in their lives. Your job is to interpret their questions and behavior and provide or look for opportunities to give information and support they need.

Using Direct, Meaningful Language

Instead of:	Say:	Because:
asleep	died	child may fear sleep
in heaven	died and/or buried	beliefs have to be explained separately
lost	died	child may continue to look for missing person or wonder why adults aren't still looking; provokes question "Wouldn't they look for me if I were lost?"
old	specific cause (such as heart attack)	age twenty seems old to a child
on a journey	died	child may fear trips
passed away	died	vagueness encourages imagination to fill in gaps, sometimes harmfully
sick	heart stopped beating; lungs wouldn't work; too sick for doctors to make well	child has difficulty distinguising between a simple cold and life-threatening illness

Use direct, meaningful language. The above chart gives suggestions for using direct language in place of the indirect or symbolic. Direct language eliminates a lot of fear and confusion for children. It allows children to develop a positive, realistic understanding of death.

Examples of Questions and Responses

Following are some examples of typical questions asked by children at different developmental stages. The actual questions children ask will depend not only on their stage of understanding but also on the level of their emotional involvement and the circumstances surrounding the specific death-related event. Remember, age ranges are not rigid. They are just reference points to indicate the steps in how children learn about death and loss. The progression is similar no matter what age range is presented.

In each set of examples, try your hand at answering the questions before reading the suggested answers. Remember also that the answers given are only examples of the responses that would be appropriate for a child's level of understanding. They are not meant to be memorized. Look at the style of language and content of the answers. Use these samples as a basis for your ideas. Put the ideas into your own words, using your own examples, feelings, and beliefs where needed. For additional samples of appropriate language, look at various children's books and note what kinds of descriptions they use. Refer to chapter 6 for a discussion of using children's literature to teach about death and loss. As long as the information is true, literature can give you a feel for appropriate language.

Typical Questions from Children under Age Three

Where is Grandpa, Mommy?
He's dead, honey. He's in heaven.
When is Grandpa coming back?
He's dead honey; he won't ever come back. We won't ever see him
    again. But we'll always miss him.
Why are you crying, Mommy?
Because Uncle Joe died today and it makes me very sad to think that
    I'll never see him again or hear him laugh.
Daddy, why won't Mommy play with me today?
Mommy is too sad to play today because her uncle died. She'll play
    with you another day. Today, I'll play with you. Let's get out the
    blocks.

Typical Questions from Children Ages Three Through Five

Why is Uncle Don so upset?
Because Grandma is dead and he won't ever see her gain.

Should I be crying too?

Only if you feel like it. Some people do and some don't. It's OK either way.

Where is Grandma?

She's dead. Her body is buried and her spirit is in heaven.

When is Grandma coming home?

She won't ever come home. She's dead and her body is buried in that cemetery over by the park.

Why did Grandma go away now? We haven't had my birthday party yet.

She didn't go away; she died. Her heart was too weak to keep beating. When your heart stops beating your body doesn't work any more and you die. I know Grandma would be sorry to miss your birthday party. We'll all miss grandma, too.

What happened to Blackie?

Blackie was in the street and a car ran over him. He's dead now.

Do rocks die when cars run over them?

No, rocks are never living so they can't die. Rocks don't breathe and move around like you and I do—like Blackie used to. But now Blackie is dead and he won't ever breathe or move around anymore.

You mean Blackie isn't going to get up and follow us home now?

No, we'll have to carry him home and have a funeral for him.

What's a funeral?

A funeral is a way people say goodbye to someone who dies. It's also a way to say how much we loved the one who died. We'll have a funeral for Blackie. I'll show you.

Why didn't Grandpa keep the lucky rabbit's foot he gave me? Then he wouldn't have to die.

Luck doesn't have anything to do with dying. Grandpa died because his whole body was so sick, for such a long time, and the doctors couldn't make him well anymore.

Aunt Martha lied to me. She promised we'd bake cookies today after school, but now she's dead.

She didn't lie to you. She didn't know she was going to die. But today, when she was coming home from the grocery store her car was hit by a big truck and the accident killed her.

Was she buying the chocolate chips at the grocery store?

I don't know. Why?

If she didn't have to get chocolate chips for our cookie baking, she wouldn't be dead.

Aunt Martha's death has nothing to do with you! She died because of a terrible accident. She bought chocolate chips for you lots of days and never had an accident before. You didn't have anything to do with the accident. Do you understand?

Yes. Now who will bake cookies with me?

I will. Today, let's bake some cookies and take them to Uncle Phil and Cousin Lynn. They must be very sad, and our cookies will remind them that we love them.

Are you sick, Daddy?

I just have a little sore throat.

Are you going to die, Daddy?

I don't expect to die until I'm a very old man. This sore throat will certainly not kill me. The doctor gave me some medicine and I'm feeling better already.

When Grandpa got sick, he took medicine and he died anyway.

I know, but Grandpa was much sicker than I am. His heart was too sick to keep beating and his lungs were too sick to keep breathing. You can live with a sore throat. You can't live without breathing lungs and a beating heart.

Why does Grandma's old room make me feel so sad?

I don't know—let's talk about it. What do you think of when you're in there?

I remember playing games and reading stories together.
Was that fun for you?
Yes.
Does anyone else play and read like Grandma did?
No.
Sounds like you're missing that special kind of fun that you had only
  with Grandma.
Yeah! I really miss Grandma—I wish she'd come back.
I know what you mean. I really miss her too. I miss her so much that
  it still makes my cry sometimes. I wish she could come back, but
  she can't. But it does make me feel better to remember our fun
  together. When I was a little girl, I used to love the way Grandma
  read *The Pokey Little Puppy.* What was your favorite story?

Typical Questions from Children Ages Six Through Eight

How did Patty's mother die?
She had cancer. The cancer cells started taking over the healthy cells
  of her body until her body just couldn't keep working anymore.
Why didn't the doctors just zap the cancer cells?
They tried several types of treatment, but it wasn't enough.
  Sometimes it works. This time it didn't.
What will happen to her body now?
Her body will be taken to a funeral home. The people there will put
  her in a casket for the funeral and burial.
Will we go to the funeral?
I will be going to the funeral. I will be going to the visitation also.
  You may go with me to the funeral or the visitation if you want to.
  Or you can stay at John's house while I go.
What do you do at a visitation?
I will visit with Patty and her family at the funeral home. Her
  mother's dead body will be there in a casket. I'll go to the casket
  and look at Patty's mother for a while—it's sort of like saying
  goodbye to her even though she can't hear us talking to her or see
  us standing there. Then I'll tell Patty and her father that I am sad

too and that I will be glad to help out if they need anything. There will be other people there doing similar things to show the family that they care.

Why is everyone dressed up (at the funeral)?
It's one of the ways we show our respect for the feelings of the family.

Why is everyone so quiet (at the funeral home)?
Some people are showing their respect; some are just thinking their own thoughts.

Why did they cut her legs off (looking at the half-open casket)?
They didn't cut her legs off. This is just a traditional way of showing the body in the casket. The legs are underneath the closed half. (If the child is close family, you may ask the funeral director to open the other half to show the child that the legs are still there.)

Why can't we see inside the casket (looking at the closed casket)?
The family decides whether the casket should be open or closed. When they decide to have it closed, it's because they think it's more respectful or because they just want to remember the dead person as they looked when they were alive instead of lying in the casket.

What is cremation?
When someone dies, some people choose to have the body put in a casket and buried in a cemetery. Others choose to have the body cremated. That means the body is burned into ashes. But remember, it doesn't hurt—the person is dead and doesn't have feelings anymore. Sometimes the ashes are kept in the family's home, and sometimes they are buried or kept in a mausoleum or crypt.

Why do we put flowers on Grandma's grave if she can't see them anymore?
Putting flowers on Grandma's grave helps us remember how much

we loved her and how much we miss her. It reminds us that she is still an important part of our lives even if she isn't with us anymore.

I haven't felt happy since Daddy died. When will I feel happy again?
I don't know when, but you will, someday. Remember, even though we're unhappy about Daddy dying, I know Daddy would want you to get back to being the happy kid you used to be. You'll still have sad times when you miss Daddy. But you'll also have memories of Daddy that will make you happy. And you'll learn to do new things and make new friends that will make you happy too.

I'm never going to speak to Aunt Doris again! If she had taken Grandpa to the hospital last night he wouldn't have died. It's all her fault!
I know you're angry about Grandpa dying. But there are two important things you need to know about what happened last night. First, Grandpa was going to die no matter what we did. His lungs were getting weaker and weaker until they finally quit working altogether. Also, Grandpa told Aunt Doris not to take him to the hospital. He didn't want a machine to breathe for him and have to live the rest of his life in a hospital bed.
You mean Grandpa wanted to die? I don't believe Grandpa would ever want to give up and die.
No, he didn't want to die. But he knew that his body wasn't capable of taking care of itself anymore. It was his time to die, and he accepted that. He didn't give up; he just understood.

Typical Questions from Children Ages Nine and Over

Will Grandpa see Grandma now that he's in heaven?
I don't know for sure, but I think that's what it's like. That's what I believe.
Why is Joe laughing? Doesn't he care that Grandpa died?
Yes, he cares. People respond in different ways. He might be laugh-

ing because he's nervous. Or he might be laughing because someone told a funny story about Grandpa, and he knows Grandpa
would want him to carry on with a happy life. People have a lot of
different emotions when they're mourning. There aren't any
wrong ones. Everyone just handles their grief the best way they
can. Do you want to tell me how you're feeling?

*How can I go ahead with my plans for my go-cart now that Uncle Phil is
dead?*
I know Uncle Phil was a big part of your plans for the go-cart rally.
But he wouldn't want you to quit now. He'd want you to find
another partner and finish what the two of you had planned. That
way it will always be something you can remember about Uncle
Phil because he got you started. What do you think?

Why doesn't anyone ever talk about Uncle Phil anymore?
Talking about Uncle Phil makes some people very sad all over again,
so they avoid it. Your father and I do talk about Uncle Phil because
we have a lot of happy memories that we want to remember. It
makes us feel good to remember the wonderful friend and brother
we used to have. I guess we've been doing our remembering when
you're not around. Would you like us to share that with you?

Why does Aunt Martha still talk about Uncle Phil all the time?
Maybe talking about Uncle Phil makes her feel like part of him is still
here. It's hard for her to be without him. Talking about him and
remembering the good times they had together makes her feel
happy. She doesn't really talk about him *all* the time. As time goes
by she'll talk about him less, but right now it's really helping her
to talk about him.

You mean someday she'll forget about him and get married to someone else?
No, she'll never forget him or the love they shared. One way to
keep the memories is to talk about them. Over time, she'll need
to talk about him less, but she'll never forget completely. She
may get married to someone else someday, but she'll still
remember Uncle Phil.

What can I do to help Cousin Lynn feel better?

Just keep being the good friend you've always been and make sure she knows we still care about her. For a while, it might be good to spend more time with her than usual. Can you think of anything special we might do to make her feel better?

Well, I know Uncle Phil used to take her for ice cream and to the park on Saturdays. Maybe we could take her now.

That's a good idea. She might not want to go with someone else. But it's a good idea to ask her about it.

5
Responding to a Recent
Death or Loss

The Stages of Grief
General Guidelines
Specific Situations

We think of most deaths as occurring within the family, but the reality is that classroom pets, teachers, classmates, and public figures die too. These deaths often have an effect on children. Like deaths, other losses can occur in any setting as well. Parents, teachers, and caregivers should be prepared to respond to deaths and losses whenever and wherever they occur.

When children are directly involved in a death or loss, they need a different type of learning strategy than those described in chapter 5. Although you still will be aware of the four basic teaching areas (facts, feelings, beliefs, and skills), your response to an actual death or loss will be more spontaneous and less structured. In your planned strategies, you had a *specific* goal for your lesson. In your responses to actual death and loss experiences, you have the *general* goal of helping a child cope with the experience positively.

> Remember, whether it's a death or other loss, we experience similar grief reactions.

You still will have to assess the child's needs. Find out what the child is feeling and how much he or she already knows. In an actual death situation, you will need to provide immediate comfort to the child. You will be teaching and role-modeling coping skills.

Instead of providing an artificial scenario, such as a story or video, you'll help children understand specific real-life situations. Depending on your relationship to the person who died, you also may be dealing with your own reactions and feelings at the same time.

If you've already used planned strategies for the child, you'll be better prepared to talk about a recent event. If you haven't, it will be important for you to be well-prepared personally to deal with death and loss concepts. If you have prepared yourself through self-assessment activities, you'll be better able to let children's needs and questions direct your responses. You'll be more open to helping them understand the full range of feelings and questions aroused by the situation—allowing them to explore their experience fully, one step at a time.

This chapter deals with that "teachable moment" when a death or loss occurs and children need help coping. It includes a discussion of typical grieving responses people—including children—go through in response to a death or loss. Remember, whether it's a death or other loss, we experience similar grief reactions. You also will find some general guidelines to assist you in helping children grieve. Finally, you will find suggestions for helping children respond to death in selected specific situations.

The Stages of Grief

According to Elisabeth Kübler-Ross (1969), a pioneer of death education, people go through five different stages in their feelings and reactions toward a death. These stages are not necessarily experienced in order, nor are they comprehensive in their description of the range of feelings. They do, however, provide a framework to use in understanding a "typical" death or loss experience.

Denial is the first stage. When first confronted with death, we often deny the facts in an attempt to give ourselves time to adjust. We might say, "No, this isn't happening to me!" We use this coping mechanism to protect ourselves. A child might say, "I know my grandma wouldn't leave without saying goodbye. She'll be back tomorrow."

The second stage often is *anger*. Once we realize we can no longer deny the facts, we become angry that this could happen to us. We might say, "Why me?" Children might say, "I hate you for saying Daddy is dead," or "I hate Daddy for dying before my big baseball game."

The third stage is *bargaining*. It is characterized by the phrase "If only . . ." Sometimes bargaining is done in the form of prayers, hoping for a miracle. Or it can be a promise to a doctor to cooperate in return for time away from treatments to visit someone special before becoming unable to travel. A child's bargain might be, "I promise to learn the multiplication tables and get one hundred percent if Mrs. Johnson can be alive today."

Next comes *depression*. When denial, anger, and bargaining fail to make situations better, children may express their depression by not eating or not playing with friends. When depression sets in, we are acknowledging the reality and finality of death. We have stopped fighting it.

As we emerge from the sadness and loneliness of depression, we begin the fifth stage—*acceptance*. Often this is a quiet, peaceful stage, somewhere between sadness and happiness. Although people may want to be left alone, they are not as lonely as they were in depression. Acceptance is a desirable state, but it can only be reached by going through the emotional stages that precede it. A child's version of acceptance might be, "I know my mother loved me. And wherever she is now, I won't ever stop loving her."

Although most people go through these five stages, they go through them at different rates, just as children's understanding develops through different levels or stages. People also may go through the first four stages in a different sequence. However, the final stage of acceptance is rarely achieved until denial, anger, bargaining, and depression have been experienced. Understanding these stages of grief can help you respond appropriately to the range of typical reactions to a death or loss.

When children deny death or loss, gentle reminders of the facts are more helpful than confrontation. When children are angry about a death, your considerate understanding is more helpful than reciprocating with your own anger. Bargaining can be dealt with by encouraging the child's expressions, even if the terms of the bargain can't be met. Depression requires acceptance of a child's need to be alone without abandoning the child entirely.

All these stages should be accepted as typical and healthy for children. Each stage has a purpose in helping the child reach the final acceptance required for readjusting to the changes in our life after a death or loss. Confronting, pressuring, returning anger, and raising false hopes can make it more difficult for children to progress through these grieving stages. Listening, reassuring, accepting, understanding, and respecting can make the process easier.

General Guidelines

Sincerity is critical when you are responding to a child's specific death or loss situation. When your responses are genuine, children can hear and feel your sincerity and will be more willing to trust you, learn from you, and be comforted by you. Some other general guidelines:

- Consider the child's perspective.
- Acknowledge losses directly.
- Involve children in death-related ceremonies.

- Provide choices for participation.
- Prepare for a variety of reactions.
- Remain aware of continuing needs.
- Consider what specific relationship has been lost.
- Know when to get professional help.

Consider the Child's Perspective

Developmentally, as discussed in chapter 2, young children have the perspective that death is not personal or final. But when they actually experience the death of a loved one or of another child, it becomes personal. In the process of their grieving, children may react with any or all of the same responses that adults do. They may deny the death, be angry about it, bargain for better circumstances, be depressed, or accept it.

Identifying where children are developmentally and which stage of grieving the child is experiencing should be a guide as you help them learn to live with the changes a death or loss brings. You *must* try to see the event from the child's perspective if you are going to be truly helpful. When you respond based only on your adult perspective or understanding, you may overreact to a child's response. You may apply adult meanings to the child's words or actions when that wasn't what the child meant at all. When you misinterpret the child's meaning, you may respond inappropriately. Or you may fail to react to something you see as trivial, when it is actually something quite important to the child.

These responses are not only confusing for children. They can cause children to turn their feelings inward and believe that adults just don't understand or don't really care about them. Don't hesitate to *ask* children for their perspective. Although they may be limited in their abilities to express themselves, if you persist you will be able to piece together clues to help you respond. Seeing a child's perspective is a difficult task with no concrete answers or assurances of success. But it's a task worth pursuing.

Acknowledge Losses Directly

Acknowledging death and loss is difficult for us as adults. Since children may be exposed to our hesitancy or denial, you may need to help them acknowledge the death and losses in their lives. Unacknowledged losses often cause children to shut down emotionally or question their own feelings. Grieving children need to be encouraged to express their feelings. Acknowledging children's feelings validates their feelings, helps them grow emotionally, and improves their self-esteem.

Involve Children in Death-Related Ceremonies

By asking, "What can we do to show how much we cared about _____?" you're encouraging children to do something but letting *them* choose *what* to do. Because children may be inexperienced at dealing with death, they may need suggestions from you for specific ways to handle the situation. By offering choices, you're providing guidance without telling them exactly how to feel or what to do. Children are able to choose actions they feel will express their individual feelings in their own ways.

How far do you go with letting children be involved? Their involvement can go as far as you can handle both emotionally and practically and as long as the children continue showing an interest. Remember, children can be involved in decision-making processes by simply being allowed to express their opinions. That doesn't mean they actually make the decisions. If you're open to letting them voice their ideas and listening to those ideas, you may be surprised at the depth of their thoughts.

When it's time to attend wakes, funerals, burials, and other memorial rituals or services, keep in mind the needs of the child and the capabilities of responsible adults. The closer the relationship between the child and the person or pet who died, the greater the need for supportive benefits that grieving rituals provide. If children will have a supportive, trusted adult available to them during a ceremony, you may let the individual children decide whether or not they will attend. If all the adults are emotionally or physically involved in the services, children should be left with people with whom they are comfortable, either at the memorial service or elsewhere.

If you aren't able to support children during services, be sure to take all opportunities to provide support after the rituals are over. As you go through pictures or the sympathy cards that have been received, you may remember parts of the service or things people said at the visitation. Share these memories with children and listen to and watch their responses. If they want to know more, you may need to describe the events completely.

If children don't ask questions, it may mean they don't have any at the moment or they don't know what to ask. They may be accepting and adapting at their own pace. In some cases, however, lack of response or question is really a hidden response. Some children are accomplished at hiding significant feelings verbally, but their *behavior* usually gives them away. If a child spends more time in Grandpa's room or looking at Grandpa's pictures than he or she does in routine daily activities, you need to talk about it. Other children might not be used to expressing emotions and feelings at all—usually due to their family's background and culture. If they become withdrawn, you might need to initiate a discussion.

If you're not sure what children are feeling or thinking, remember your first step can always be to ask them. If they're unsure, your next step can be to read stories in children's books to find examples. Ask children if their feelings are similar to or different from the character's feelings. Sometimes it's helpful to share your own feelings to let children see that it really is OK to say things out loud. (Refer to chapter 6 for further discussion on using children's stories.)

If you're still not getting feedback to help you understand children's needs, check with others who spend time with them. This means that parents ask teachers and teachers ask parents and other significant adults. If your attempts don't seem to be working and you still have concerns about a child's attitude or behavior, seek professional help.

Provide Choices for Participation

When you choose to express your sympathy with a card, flowers, or donation, resist the urge to simply sign the names of children without talking to them. If children show little interest, signing their names is acceptable. But if they ask questions or show interest, let them get more involved. You might share your feelings about why you are sending the card, flowers, or donation. Children also can be involved in making or choosing memorial gifts or just sitting and listening as family members choose music for the funeral. Adults can use these opportunities to share and explain beliefs.

Consider other options for involving children as well. They might help select, pick, or arrange flowers. They can make sympathy cards, draw pictures, or write letters in memory of a loved one. Depending on the location, children can take flowers to a grave after a ceremony or ride by and visit on a bike ride. For example, older children might visit a grave or some other place that reminds them of their dead grandmother in much the same way that adults do—carrying on a one-sided conversation, asking for advice, or sharing their feelings with Grandma. When children sing songs that remind them of Grandpa or continue with a hobby that Grandpa helped them start, it's another way of coping with loss and honoring the loved one.

Prepare for a Variety of Reactions

Children who have had a close relationship with a person who died usually will choose a way to acknowledge the death both as a memorial and for their own need to be involved in remembering and honoring the person. Children with less substantial relationships may not need to take action because the death hasn't caused as much of a loss. Children's reactions will vary. But if you have provided children with facts, a comfortable environment for their exploration, and choices for their expressions, you've prepared well.

Remain Aware of Continuing Needs

After the ceremonies are over, continue watching carefully as children readjust to life without the loved one. Watch for signs of understanding, lingering questions, and the need for professional help. If children aren't "acting like themselves," their body language or behaviors indicate that something's wrong. If they aren't telling you what's wrong or how they feel, you may need to help them bring death or loss out in the open so you can explore it together.

Children's books, music, and movies are good discussion starters (see chapter 6). For example, after reading a story about a family whose grandparent died, you can ask questions and make comments to help children express their own feelings, beliefs, memories, or needs. This activity helps move children from the general sense of loss to specific situations or feelings that they can agree with, disagree with, feel good about, feel sad about, or show any combination of feelings about. Whatever their response, they're expressing their own views or questions and are taking small steps toward understanding and acceptance.

Consider What Specific Relationship Has Been Lost

Children's perspectives and relationships to the object lost or the person who died will influence their responses. Discussions of the experience must be left open-ended so children can lead you where they need to go. For example, if a pet dies, children may be concerned about the burial and possibly a memorial service. If a parent dies, children are less likely to be concerned with rituals and more likely to be concerned about their own emotions or their own future security. If you're unsure about the children's concerns, remember to ask them.

Know When to Get Professional Help

Just as you yourself respond to a variety of current experiences, you need to be aware of the variety of experiences and reactions of children. Learn how to identify whether this is a time for comfort and teaching or a time for professional counseling. Initially, you may think that your support and teaching are enough then find, through your interactions, that professional help is needed.

The best guides for knowing when to get professional help are your own intuition and your knowledge of the individual child. In general, what you're looking for is *any change* in typical behavior that lasts, such as:

- not wanting to play with friends or refusing favorite activities,
- not wanting to eat or refusing favorite foods,
- being unable to sleep or to sleep alone,
- having nightmares that persist,
- having recurring stomachaches with no physical cause.

Any or all of these behaviors can be acceptable for a limited time. They are common symptoms of grieving. The determining factors are whether the behavior is a change from a child's typical behavior before the death or loss and whether it persists, keeping the child from readjusting to life after the loss.

Specific Situations

Some examples of specific death and loss situations are presented here. Suggested responses are discussed for each situation. Remember that these are *sample* responses. Adapt the concepts and phrases to fit your situations, your personal style, your cultural background and beliefs, your own language, and the individual child.

When a Special Toy Is Lost

When a young child loses an object that he or she is especially attached to—like a blanket or a teddy bear—it is an important loss in the life of that child. From an adult perspective, "It's only a stuffed toy." But from a child's perspective, "It's my sense of comfort, my confidant, my best friend, my protector while I sleep," and so on. To understand a child's perspective, think how you would feel if your best friend moved to a distant country or even died. It gives you a different feeling, doesn't it?

Begin by stating the facts in a way that shows your respect for the seriousness of the situation and your acceptance of the child's feelings. Say, for example, "I'm so sorry we left Boo-Bear in the hotel. But when we called the hotel manager, he said they didn't find anything. We can't fly back to Oregon to look for him." All of these comments acknowledge the child's traumatic response and clarify any details or boundaries.

> Remember to share both the good-feeling memories and the feelings of loss. Show your respect and acceptance.

For a less severe response to a lost toy, simply acknowledging the loss and sadness may be enough. You'll know if you're taking the right approach by listening sensitively to the child's comments and feelings. If you're in tune with the child's perspective, you'll hear the importance of his or her words.

If further actions are necessary, provide choices. You might suggest trying to

Responding to a Recent Death or Loss

have another stuffed toy try to do Boo-Bear's job, since Boo-Bear isn't with us any more. If you suggest such a replacement, be sure to acknowledge that it won't be the same as Boo-Bear but that it might make the child feel better. Some children may still reject a replacement. If so, offer other choices. Sometimes a parent can lie down with a child for a few nights until the child learns that he or she will be okay without the bear. Or ask the child for suggestions about what will make him or her feel better.

As pictures or memories show up with Boo-Bear in them, remember to share both the good-feeling memories and the feelings of loss. Show your respect and acceptance. When you keep the subject open for discussion, you allow children a chance to practice experiencing unpleasant or difficult feelings in a supportive environment.

When Parents Separate or Divorce or Children Must Move

When parents separate, divorce, or change jobs, children often have to move to a new home. They experience many different types of losses when they change homes. We can easily understand the loss of routines, neighborhoods, bedrooms, and friends. But what about a child who is upset about leaving new bedroom wallpaper? Is this trivial? Maybe to you, as an adult, but if the child expresses this loss, you need to acknowledge and respect it. Later, you may find a deeper underlying reason for the concern about the wallpaper—the special time the child had while helping Dad put the paper on the walls, for example. But even if you don't understand what might be behind a child's expressed concern, respect it anyway. You can't move the bedroom with you, but you can listen and care about the child's feelings.

When parents divorce, in addition to physical losses, children may be experiencing the loss of the parent who played the role of confidant, or birthday cake baker, or ballplayer, or piano teacher. To make things worse, these losses for the children come at a time when the custodial parent's strengths are reduced due to the stress of the divorce. If, on the other hand, a child's relationship with the parent who leaves the home was never very strong, the child's losses may center on physical losses with only limited personal or relationship losses.

In the critical situation of an abusive parent leaving or being removed, a child may experience relief and even joy. At this time, it's important to remain watchful for feelings of guilt. Children need persistent reassurance that they are not responsible for adults' actions.

To prepare children for various losses, explain as much as possible the details that will affect the children. Offer suggestions for ways to ease the process. If you have a custody schedule worked out, tell children when they will be with each parent. You might suggest that the child carry both parents' phone numbers so they can both be reached almost any time. These efforts provide predictability that helps children feel more secure.

Include as much hands-on and active involvement as possible. Use a calendar, even for small children, to make the schedule more concrete and easier to understand. If children have to move, let them go along when house- or apartment-hunting and listen to their opinions. Remember that you don't have to act on their preferences, but listen to them, and you might hear about something that will help them adjust.

Clarify which objects or furnishings will be moved and which might have to stay behind. If children will change schools, let them know what school they'll be attending as soon as you know. You can offer to go to the new school to meet the new teacher. You also might suggest visiting friends from the old school on weekends, talking to them by telephone, or both. Try to keep surprises to a minimum. Be honest and direct about whatever details children show an interest in and those that will affect them directly.

Keep your lines of communication as open as possible, respect the children's perspective, acknowledge their feelings, and provide helpful suggestions. Even when you prepare and support as much as you can, however, don't expect children to accept changes instantly or easily. Just as new pets can't replace the old ones, new friends, new rooms, and new stepparents can't replace the old ones.

Allow children to talk about their old neighborhood and school or have pictures around as reminders. Maybe you miss your garden at the old house or one of your children's old friends being around. Share these feelings with your children.

Pictures and memories help children gradually let go of the old ways and adjust to new ways at their own pace. As always, if you don't see children making progress toward adjusting to life changes, they may need professional help. But if children are adapting, however slowly, keep praising their adjustments and encouraging them to keep taking new steps.

When a Pet Dies

One common early death experience for children is the death or loss of a pet. As with any death or loss experience, circumstances will vary and so will children's reactions. Although your responses can't be stated specifically for all situations, there are some general guidelines that can be helpful.

First, acknowledge the death of a pet directly. Resist the urge to replace a goldfish or hamster when the child isn't looking. Remember that it's much more frightening to think that a living creature can just disappear without notice or caring than it is to acknowledge a pet's death and related emotions. Begin by telling children the basic facts. The pet died. When did it die? If you know the cause, tell about it. Knowing the cause often helps children accept the death.

Remember that children's reactions to each death will differ depending on their relationship with the pet. If they were responsible for its care and had close daily contact, their reactions will be strongest. But even the strongest reactions may vary from anger to sadness to guilt—particularly if the care of the pet was their responsibility. They'll also have different reactions depending on previous experiences with death or loss as well as on their stage of development or level of understanding. If they don't understand the finality of death when it occurs, they will come to understand as time goes by (because, for instance, the dog never returns) and will develop mental abilities to realize that death is permanent.

Once you've acknowledged the pet's death, let children take the next step. Listen to their comments and questions for clues to help you understand how significant the event is for them. Offer suggestions, but don't force them or yourself into specific responses. For example, if the death doesn't seem terribly upsetting, you might say, "Would you like me to take care of burying

Goldie for you, or would you like to help?" On the other hand, if the death is very upsetting, you might be more directive by saying, "What can we do to show how much we cared for Goldie?"

What if a pet is lost or missing instead of dead? You still have to deal with the circumstances directly and honestly. If you know when the pet left or what direction it headed, share this information with the children. Don't pretend the dog is missing when you know it is dead. But if you don't know it is dead, be honest about that, too. It's OK to say, "I don't know if Fido just wandered off and got lost or got killed by a car."

Once you've shared what you know, allow children time to ask questions and share feelings. Be prepared for a variety of responses from disinterested to inconsolable. Honest communication builds the strongest foundation for further exploration of a situation and the range of emotions that may result.

As children share their responses with you, begin offering practical suggestions. Maybe you can conduct a neighborhood search, or call the animal shelter, or make "lost cat" posters for area bulletin boards. If it's too late at night, you may have to wait until morning to take further actions. If children are responding emotionally, acknowledge that it may be difficult to sleep, but explain that the search will be safer and easier in the daylight.

It is important to let children be as actively involved as possible. Involvement can mean doing something to just being included in knowing all the facts. Whatever form it takes, involvement is one of the keys to coping effectively with death and loss.

If it turns out that the pet is dead, children may want to have a funeral, a burial, or both. When it's their choice, this is a good idea. If you're in a rural area with plenty of open spaces, the burial probably won't create any problems. If you're in an urban area, space or regulations may rule out a burial. A goldfish or hamster is easy to bury because it doesn't require a large space or a deep grave. But a cat or dog is more difficult. You may need to suggest that the veterinarian cremate your pet (if this method fits your belief system). Then, you can have a funeral or memorial service but no burial.

Whenever possible, let children decide how the service will take place. If they ask you a question about the burial or ceremony, try to respond with choices. Sometimes you may have to limit the children's options based on what you're willing, able, or allowed to do. You may have city regulations that must be followed or personal time constraints.

But whenever possible, give children choices. For example, "One of you could carry the box with Goldie in it, or we could put it in the wagon and pull it out to the grave site." Or, "We could bury Rusty back by the fence, or we could take him to the vet and ask the vet to cremate him for us."

If you're at home and you feel that a prayer is appropriate, say one. If you're at school where children bring ideas from different cultures and religions, let them mix up their rituals in whatever ways they choose. The whole purpose of the activity is for children to express their reaction to the death, honor the dead pet, and make the death real by making a physical and verbal good-bye.

Remember that initial urge to simply replace the pet? You know it shouldn't be done secretly. Should it be done at all? This answer will be a familiar: whenever you can, let children decide. When they ask for a new hamster, that's a good time to discuss it. You may have to explain that a new pet won't be possible due to space or money. Or you may discuss what type of pet to get and where to get it.

In general, getting a new pet immediately is not a good idea because this might lead the child to believe that one being can be replaced by another. "Does that mean I can be replaced?" This is uncomfortable and possibly frightening. Make sure children understand that a new pet may be fun and that we'll learn to love it but that the new pet won't be the same as Rusty and that we won't care for Rusty any less.

When a Grandparent Dies

If children are told the facts about the death of a grandparent, then listened to and comforted at home, they may be able to cope with their feelings well enough so that teachers never find out about the death. This is especially possible if the grandparent didn't live nearby or if the child had only a distant or occasional relationship with the grandparent.

But if the child was raised by the grandparent or had a similar close relationship, a child's responses are likely to occur at home and at school. In both settings, children want their feelings to be respected and accepted. Listen carefully, then share your own feelings and beliefs.

If you're talking to children at home, you may have all the facts needed to share with the children. If you're talking to children at school, you may not know the facts. In that case, you may be responding to questions from the children to help them understand facts they've been told. You may need to help them decide what questions they want to ask when they get home. You might begin by asking children what they know or feel about the death. Then follow the general guidelines at the beginning of this chapter. When teachers, parents, and caregivers share details of a child's death or loss experience, the child benefits from the comfort of consistent information.

When a Teacher or Public Figure Dies

When a teacher or a public figure dies, younger children may display their self-centeredness by completely ignoring the event. Even though the whole community may be talking about it, if children didn't really know the person who died, they may go on with their daily routines unaffected. If their teacher (or neighbor) dies, however, they may need help coping with the event.

Children's concerns might sound like these: "Who will be our new teacher?" "Will our new teacher take us to the fire department next Friday like we planned?" "I wish I hadn't been so mean to Mr. Smith before he died." "I hope our next teacher is more fun than Miss Jones. I never liked her." "Why is Billy still so sad? Mr. Smith died a long time ago, and I like Miss Goodman better anyway." "Now we can get a new *nice* neighbor."

Depending on the child's perspective, he or she may need to be reassured that new routines can be learned and that any feelings—except guilt—are acceptable. Explain that some things like lunchtime and gym class will be the same as before. The new teacher may have a different way of doing show-and-tell or assigning homework. The new neighbor could become a friend. Let children know what you know, and help them learn ways of finding out new information for themselves. You might suggest that being nice to teachers is important, but liking teachers is not necessary. It's also OK if one child's opinion or perspective is different from another's. Children's individual relationships with the teacher or neighbor were different. Their responses will be different too.

When the person who dies is a public person (for example, a president) or when many people die at one time, the school, neighborhood, and media will be talking about the death. In these circumstances, children often overhear more than they can understand. Be aware when children are listening. Make sure you use honest and direct language as described in chapter 4. Give children an opportunity to ask questions so you can be sure of how much they understand and whether they have all the information they need.

When a public figure dies, communities often organize a public memorial. This brings the death to the attention of more people and involves more people—including children—in the memorial rituals. These are excellent opportunities for children to witness the variety of responses (both emotional and practical) that people have to death.

If you want to discuss any aspect of the death that might cause unnecessary fear or confusion for children, have your discussion away from the children. Remember that although we don't want to hide death from children, we also don't want to give them more information than they can cope with or understand.

If the death is due to AIDS or another serious chronic condition, you may discuss the cause and possibly begin a discussion about prevention. But there is no need to discuss the details of the person's physical deterioration. Fear of AIDS or cancer as deadly diseases is enough reality. Fear of the symptoms and side-effects isn't necessary to understanding, coping with, and readjusting after the death.

A school may plant a memorial tree or have a memorial service or moment of silence to honor a teacher. Communities may organize ringing of all church bells in unison at the beginning of the funeral. Newspapers may print eulogies written by residents to honor community philanthropists or leaders. When you're considering your own participation in these events, remember to offer a role to your children.

Children who are interested in or need to be involved in these grieving and memorial rituals can participate in any of the strategies listed above. When children are strongly affected, they may have specific ideas of their own about how they want to participate. Since children often don't feel bound by social conventions, they may provide fresh insights and excellent suggestions.

Because the death of a public figure affects so many people in one community and is likely to have media coverage, the event may remain in people's minds longer than the death of a lesser-known person. As children see a new neighbor or learn the expectations of a new teacher, they come across daily reminders of the dead neighbor or teacher. Each time a routine is changed, they're reminded of how it used to be. Continue listening and watching for clues to children's coping abilities as long as needed. Encourage positive coping skills, like reminiscing over pictures or stories. Get additional help if you note reactions that you think might harm a child's development:for example, feelings of guilt or extended lack of interest in other activities or people.

When a Parent Dies

When a parent dies, a child's perspective probably centers on his or her own security. Your role as the surviving parent, relative, teacher, or friend is to provide as much reassurance as possible. Don't tell children everything will be OK—of course things won't be OK without their parent. But do tell them who will fix their breakfast, take them to baseball practice, stay home with them when they are sick, or read them a bedtime story.

Let them know that you understand it won't be the same but that they will be taken care of. Even when you don't have an answer, remember that the truth is more reassuring than false hope that can backfire. When you don't know an answer, offer to find out, help them find out, or promise to tell them whenever you find out. This honest communication allows children to feel included as much as possible.

What if the parent/child relationship was not a warm, supportive, healthy one? What if it was abusive? The same security issues usually arise. Since young children often don't know there is another way of life (that is, not abusive), they think everyone has a similar lifestyle. They still love their parents and look to them for security.

In most cases, your responses will be the same, regardless of the quality of the parent/child relationship. In some cases, however, older children may feel guilty or relieved about the death of an abusive parent. When these emotions are observed or heard, consider professional support. These are long-term, complex issues that won't be completely resolved by comfort and teaching.

Within the home, the death of a parent must be acknowledged immediately. If it's not a sudden death, it's best to begin talking about the death before it happens. Acknowledge death by sharing honest facts, beliefs, and feelings. Facts help children accept reality, while beliefs and feelings help them express, explore,

Responding to a Recent Death or Loss

and grieve for the loss. These processes help children develop the coping skills necessary for living with death and loss.

At school or church, it may be tempting to avoid discussion about the death of a child's parent. But you're not bringing up the subject of death in this case—you're all thinking about it anyway. What you are doing is acknowledging the importance of the loss and providing some support and a role model to help children learn to cope with realities.

> Even when you don't have an answer, remember that the truth is more reassuring than false hope that can backfire.

This can be a time of additional bonding for the surviving parent or caregiver and children. Take this opportunity to include children in as many activities and decisions as you can. It will not be easy, but all difficult tasks are made easier when shared with a loved one. If you're concerned about whether children should go with you to choose a gravestone, consider asking children if they'd like to go. If this seems too difficult, tell children why you have to go alone. Then, make sure they have caring adults and a comfortable place to wait for your return.

Regarding the funeral or other ceremonies, it is more important for children to attend when it is their own parent who has died. You need to push yourself to either handle the children's needs or find someone you and your children trust to be their comforter. Children should be encouraged but not forced to attend services. Force just adds another level of stress that is unnecessary.

While offering a choice, adults can still encourage children to attend by describing the supportive benefits and by assuring children that they will be cared for during the process. You may simply state that you will feel better if the children you love are with you or that they don't have to look at the body.

If the funeral is for a friend's parent, attending funeral services is less critical to children's acceptance of finality. The death may be further removed, and children can be offered a choice with less direction from adults. The closer the relationship, the greater the need for the finality and support provided by death-related ceremonies.

Ceremonies are usually over within a few days. But children have a long-range task of adjusting to life without a parent. They are almost sure to find daily reminders of the parent throughout the home and their routines. Each daily reminder, regardless of size or significance, constitutes a specific loss that needs to be acknowledged directly and honestly, just as the death itself was.

As you continue to deal with each loss, be alert to children's ongoing need for support and your own need for personal support and help with your children. As you teach children to ask for support and express their feelings, remember to follow your own advice. Seek assistance for yourself too. Ask your friends and relatives to help keep an eye on children's readjustment. Your eyes may be too clouded with your own grief to see your children's need clearly.

In addition to daily reminders, each holiday or special occasion probably will renew the memory of the loss. Holiday traditions are a powerful part of children's sense of security. It is difficult to let go of the comfort of the old traditions and adjust to or develop new traditions.

Although we want children to get on with their new life without a parent, we can't expect them to do it easily. Use holidays to remember old ways. Remember the way Mom used to hide the birthday cake so it would be a surprise? Or the way Dad always sang when he put on the holiday lights? Talk to children to see if they want to keep up some of the old practices or leave them as special memories. They may want everyone to sing as the lights are put on, in honor of Dad. Or they may not want singing because it interferes with their pleasant memories. Different children find comfort in different ways, just as adults do. The appropriate response is the one that most helps a particular child.

If you find that children aren't getting on with celebrating or playing or learning or loving in their lives, consider professional counseling. Don't let the death of a parent prevent a healthy life for a child. Don't blame yourself for a child's inability to readjust. When the steps you've taken seem inadequate or when a child stops growing and developing, it is a time to take positive action, not a time to blame.

In the case of an abusive parent's death, once children find a new sense of security without the abusive parent, they may begin to confront their feelings about the abuse. They may realize that they actually feel better without the parent in their lives. The complexity and depth of these awakenings require more than a supportive environment. You haven't failed unless you fail to be concerned about the children's welfare. Continue to seek professional help for them.

When a Child Dies

An elderly person's death fits with our view of the natural order of things; a child's death does not. This is not just an adult perspective. Even children who have come along way toward understanding that death is final, unavoidable, and inevitable still believe that it happens to grown-ups, not children. This concept is one of the last to develop in children.

Developmentally, this means that children aren't really ready to conceive of their own deaths. Then what happens to a child's perspective when another child dies? Some children will totally block out the event. They will refuse to think about it. This may be a mechanism for self-preservation. The child may simply be unable to handle the information at this time.

Other children will make an instant jump into a new and frightening level of awareness—that death is *personal*. Although they weren't developmentally ready to take in this information, real-life circumstances have forced them to be more grown-up. As a result, the greatest degree of support may be needed when another child dies.

With supportive adults in their lives, children can learn to cope with their new knowledge and feelings. It will take some longer than others, but they will learn. As with other deaths, the closeness of the relationship between the surviving child and the one who died will affect the way the child deals with the death.

Although children can't be pushed into acceptance and understanding of the death of another child, the circumstances must be dealt with directly and honestly. Be open to children's questions and concerns. Provide answers and support as they follow their own pace toward understanding.

Because of children's developmental levels and their emotional involvement, it may take longer to accept the death of a child than any other death. You can help by acknowledging the death and clarifying the circumstance of the death.

It is important to help children see how they are different from the child who died and also how they are similar. For example, if a child dies of leukemia and the children you are working with are not cancer patients, you can point out your children's health as a difference in this particular situation. If a child is hit by a car or dies from an overdose of drugs, use this as a teaching opportunity in addition to providing emotional support to the children.

Gently, over time, you can help children understand. Help them find ways to be involved, such as participating in a school memorial or writing notes to the parents of the child who died. Although some parents will reject overtures from other children attempting to console them, others will be touched and comforted by the children's actions. Prepare children for possible negative reactions from the parents of the dead child. But remember that the purpose of the activity is to help the *children* work through their feelings. If these are true gestures from the hearts of the children, they are likely to be accepted as such.

There are some situations where children are likely to need professional help in adjusting to the death of another child: if they witness an accidental death; if the death is violent; if children shared an accident or traumatic event and some died while some lived. Also, if similarities between the child who died and surviving children are significant, children may be too fearful to cope with the death without assistance from trained professionals. Don't forget that they'll still need your support in addition to whatever professional support they receive.

As time goes by, you can help just by sharing children's memories. Listen to their stories, help them care for a keepsake item, or watch the annual budding of the memorial tree together. Be available to address the death over the long term. As children grow in their ability to understand death, they will need to revisit specific experiences. Shared memories and activities are excellent ways to help children see a death through the light of their own new understanding. Remember not to suggest that new friends take the place of old ones. We don't *replace* human beings in our lives. But we can encourage children to enjoy new friendships in addition to remembering the old one.

When the Death Is Sudden and Violent

Children are bombarded on a daily basis with images of sudden violent death—fatal automobile crashes, drive-by shootings, bombings, other homicides, and suicides—through newspapers, television, movies, the internet, and other media. Children also can become aware of these kinds of deaths through planned strategies like those described in chapter 6. None of these experiences, however, can ever prepare children for the sudden death of a loved one or the violent death of someone they have known. In fact, no child or adult could ever be prepared for such violence as our whole country experienced when terrorists flew airplanes into the World Trade Center towers and the Pentagon on September 11, 2001. One thing, however, remains true. Regardless of how difficult it is for adults, we must be consistent informers, comforters, interpreters, and advocates for children.

Children must go through the same stages of grief when dealing with these tragic sudden deaths: denial, anger, bargaining, depression, and acceptance. They also experience tremendous shock with no time to prepare or adjust. They may need more help, guidance, and time to deal with an unexpected death, particularly if it was violent. Like adults, children may go through a period of emotional numbness followed by feelings of resentment, anger, loneliness, guilt, hurt, blame, and sadness.

Violent death also may bring about feelings of anxiety and fear for safety. A drive-by shooting, a rape, or a drug overdose may confirm a child's perceptions about dangers in the neighborhood. A suicide committed by a classmate may confirm a child's perceptions that his or her future is hopeless and that the only way to deal with that hopelessness is to take one's own life. A suicide committed by a parent may provide an incorrect model for dealing with life's problems. The brutal death of three friends in an automobile crash may confirm a young child's fear of riding to the supermarket with his or her parents. Terrorist attacks, school shootings, and war may create fears in any or all areas of children's lives, including obvious concerns as well as concerns that we have never imagined before.

As soon as possible, reassure children about their safety. Honesty is the foundation of this conversation. Although you may not be able to assure complete safety, you can identify specific areas of safety and any new routines or actions that are being taken to improve their safety. Parents and teachers can help children deal with violent deaths by providing them with understanding, comfort, and accurate information. Remember, what you say and how you say it will depend on the child's developmental stage, emotional state, and belief system.

Explain what happened, but don't feel obligated to give a graphic description. Make sure the information is accurate. In most cases, when a violent death occurs, inaccurate rumors lead to unnecessary panic and anxiety. If the deceased was a student or teacher in the child's school, acknowledge the death and be sensitive to the child's need to talk about it.

Some schools have a crisis response system to respond to the death of a student or staff member. This organized response often enables students and staff to return to emotional normality sooner. Although school plans may vary from site to site, the primary purposes are

- to provide accurate information for all students and staff;
- to allay unnecessary fears by creating a safe, secure environment; and
- to provide emotional support for those most closely associated with the person or persons who died.

The response system may include writing letters to parents and other community members, allowing teachers and students to attend funeral services, doing something for the immediate family, providing small-group counseling for students and staff, and planning a school memorial.

6
Using Planned Learning Strategies and Children's Literature

Choosing Appropriate Strategies
Preparing Yourself
Getting Started
Emphasizing Lessons Learned
Teaching Strategies about Facts
Teaching Strategies about Beliefs
Teaching Strategies about Feelings
Teaching Strategies about Coping Skills
Choosing and Using Children's Literature

Parents, caregivers, and teachers can create opportunities to teach children about death and loss. This chapter offers suggestions for preparing and using planned learning activities and children's literature to address issues related to death and loss. Teachers will be more likely to use these planned programs. Parents and caregivers might also use these ideas to help them begin conversations with their children. First, you'll find a discussion of appropriate activities, then ways to prepare for activities you choose. Next, there are key concepts to emphasize about the lessons learned in each activity. The final sections include brief descriptions of activities grouped by topic area—facts, feelings, beliefs, and coping skills.

These strategies are arranged based on their primary focus. There is overlap, however, among the topics. Use these suggested activities as a source of ideas. They will help you discover the variety of ways you can present death and loss in learning strategies for children.

Choosing Appropriate Strategies

Because of your special understanding of the children with whom you work, you're the best person to judge which strategies to use and when. The general suggestions below will help you make decisions and prepare for using the learning strategies.

As you already know, for the lesson to be effective, children must be able to understand the lesson you have planned. Think about the developmental level of the children. How many steps have your children already taken, and what step can they take next? Remember, when you refer to the stages described in chapter 2, age is not necessarily the best indicator; rather, age is just a reference point. The sequence of steps taken and a child's previous experiences are what you should consider when evaluating children's readiness for a lesson.

Sequence of strategies is as important for you as it is for children. When you're comfortable with conversations about death and loss, you can create an open environment children need to explore freely. It may be helpful to start with the less emotional activities about facts and beliefs. As you get a feel for children's abilities to understand and cope with death and loss, you'll become aware of your own ability to manage sensitive issues. As you and your child become more comfortable, you can progress to more abstract and emotional activities about feelings and coping skills.

In addition to sequence and the developmental level of the activity, you'll be deciding on appropriate topic areas. Do children need to understand facts or do they need to learn to express feelings? Should you teach about beliefs or coping skills? These questions are easier to answer when children bring up death and loss themselves. If they are expressing feelings, you respond with feeling-oriented strategies. If they are asking concrete questions, you respond with fact-oriented strategies.

When you're planning a sequence of activities unrelated to a specific event, it's a little more complicated. The decision depends on the children involved. Some children are comfortable with and experienced in expressing feelings. Others may need concrete facts before they will be able to explore feelings that facts arouse. For a sequence of planned strategies, a general guideline would be to begin with facts and beliefs, follow up with feelings, then move to coping skills.

Preparing Yourself

Once you've decided on the developmental level and topic area, prepare appropriate materials and environment for the activity. You might provide some starter ideas for children in some strategies. In other strategies, you may decide to leave the activity open-ended, allowing children's involvement and interests to determine the direction of discussion. In formal settings, as with other sensitive topics, check school district, agency, or other policies about guidelines for informing parents before implementing any of the strategies.

Some strategies can be used in more than one way—focused on either children's feelings or children's knowledge about death-related concepts. Choose one focus or the other. Remember to let the children explore one step at a time. Most important, remember that the strategies presented are just suggestions. Adapt them to meet your own needs and style. You are best qualified to make decisions about topics and techniques. You are the one who knows what you can handle, what your children can handle, and how much time you have available for the activity and any necessary follow-up.

At the end of this chapter, you'll find suggestions on selecting and using children's stories to teach about death and loss. Some of the same tips apply when evaluating and selecting a video. You must do more than preview your materials. Make sure you know the video or book content, dialogue, and images very well.

When you're previewing, pay attention to the particular details you want to focus on. Be aware of any feelings that might be aroused in children or in yourself. Identify any information that might present a biased view. Biased material might still be useful provided you're aware of the slant and can compensate for it.

Since children will surprise you with their responses, consider as many possible responses as you can. If you feel you need more background information to tackle an activity, use the references and additional readings listed at the back of the book to help you with your research.

Death and loss learning strategies at school and other formal settings may also arouse emotions in parents and caregivers. If discussing death and loss are not recommended by your district guidelines, consider sending a note home letting adults know about the strategies you have planned. This notification is more than just a courtesy to help parents and caregivers prepare for questions children bring home. If parents are prepared, they may be more open. Children then have the double benefit of an open environment at school and at home.

Getting Started

Before beginning a strategy, introduce the topic and strategy to the children. Let them know what will take place during the strategy. For example, "We'll read a story, then we'll do some pretending and some artwork to help us think about our feelings." When the topic is feelings or beliefs, consider using some of the following kinds of statements when introducing the strategy:

- This strategy deals with feelings about death and loss in your life.
- There are no right or wrong answers. All your feelings are OK.
- Don't worry about agreeing with someone else's answers. Just think about your own feelings.
- The important part of the activity is for you to find out how you feel about deaths and losses in your life.

If the story is very sad or if a child in your group has had a similar experience, some children may become upset and even cry. If you think this response is possible, you will want to discuss it before you begin the strategy. Maybe younger children can get a comforting stuffed toy or blanket to hold during a story. Remind children that it's OK to feel sad, to cry, or even not to feel sad. All their feelings are OK. Explain that teachers, other children, parents, or caregivers will be glad to give hugs as needed. You may have your own special way of dealing with this issue. Just be sure children feel as safe and comfortable as possible.

Even when activities are discussed, have children give their written work or art to you. When you review it, you can see any reactions that weren't brought up in discussion. If there are products from the activity, such as essays or pictures, display them at home or school. Consider including a description of the strategy and children's responses in a newsletter to parents (if you are a teacher) or a note to a teacher (if you are a parent or caregiver). When parents, caregivers, and teachers are communicating and working together, the environment for a child's exploration is expanded.

Emphasizing Lessons Learned

Your discussion may bring out additional ideas. Be sure to include them when summarizing or emphasizing lessons learned. As you end a strategy, consider comments to children like the following. Remember to change the ideas into your own words as needed. Select comments most suited to the appropriate development level of your children.

- Thank you for sharing your feelings.
- Talking about death and loss can be hard sometimes. Maybe this activity will make it easier for you to talk about these things on another day.
- We talked about many different feelings.
- All of your feelings are important.
- Your feelings and beliefs make you unique or special.
- It's important for you to take time to think about how you feel.
- Maybe you changed your ideas as you listened to others describe what they thought. Or maybe you realized how strongly you feel or believe in something because you weren't willing to change your views.
- It's important to understand your own feelings and feelings of others. You don't have to agree with others, but understanding what they think can be interesting and helpful.
- Maybe you've thought of some questions that you want to ask other adults. Who do you want to ask?
- If you think of some new questions or feelings tomorrow or another day, we can talk about them some more. All you have to do is ask.
- Feelings are an important part of us.
- You did a nice job of sharing your feelings and listening to others' feelings.
- It's important to share our feelings with others. Sometimes it can make us feel less sad or lonely. Sometimes it can help us remember a special happiness.
- It's important to care about the feelings of others.
- Sometimes we think that only "good" feelings are OK. But that's not true. All our feelings are an important part of us. Sometimes the feelings we think are "bad" turn out not to be so bad when we say them out loud.
- Things we do can be "bad" if they hurt another person. But our feelings aren't "bad." For example, if we're really mad at someone, it's OK to be really mad. But it's not OK to hit the person.

Try not to leave children with unanswered questions or unclarified concepts. (Refer to the section on teaching facts in chapter 3 for advice on finding clues to a child's understanding.) Remember that children may try to fill in gaps by using their imaginations. Make sure you ask questions to check their understanding. Give them opportunities to ask questions to clarify for themselves. In addition to being clear, it's a good idea to end a strategy by reinforcing important messages it teaches.

Teaching Strategies about Facts

Word Games

This strategy is designed to help clarify concepts for children in the stages typical of ages six through eight and ages nine and over. It can help them develop the *vocabulary* needed to ask questions and learn facts related to death and loss. When preparing for this strategy, familiarize yourself with as many terms and definitions as you can.

Ask children to help you make a list of words they hear when people are talking about death and loss (for example, "wake" and "cremation"). Write down the words as children say them. Follow up by discussing all the words until an accurate definition is clearly formed for each. You may want to divide children into small groups or pairs to come up with their own definitions of words before you discuss and clarify definitions as a whole group. A crossword puzzle or word search puzzle makes a good closing or review.

Consider these possible variations: For older children, you could list various beliefs about life after death or beliefs regarding funeral rituals. (See the activity in chapter 1 on cultural traditions and religious beliefs for samples or idea starters). Follow-up would include the same type of clarifying and defining. Remember—no judgment, just description. This follow-up strategy could be used after a reading assignment, defining key terms in the assignment.

When closing an activity, stress the importance of learning to use words correctly so that people can ask questions and better understand death- and loss-related concepts.

Cemetery Visit

Children in the stages typical of ages six through eight and ages nine and over can benefit from this strategy. The goal is to teach children about the *different ways people bury their loved ones.* Parents and caregivers may make an informal visit to

a cemetery, possibly a cemetery where relatives are buried. Teachers may schedule a formal field trip, following school district guidelines for such trips.

To prepare for the trip, visit the cemetery yourself first. Take a walk around the grounds and decide on specific things to point out to children. To prepare children, tell them where you're going and what they'll be seeing. Give children time to talk about what they know about cemeteries and ask questions. Try to find out whether anyone is afraid of the trip or if anyone knows someone buried in the cemetery you'll be visiting.

Spring is a good time for this outdoor field trip because of weather and because cemeteries often are naturally pretty during this season. When things are bright and growing, it becomes less somber, allowing children to think about the physical details you want to teach.

If you can provide additional adult chaperones, you will have the option of dividing the group into smaller groups for exploring. Be sure to make a list of details you want the other adults to point out to children in each group.

Check with the groundskeeper or cemetery manager to schedule your visit. If a funeral is scheduled, they will inform you. Respect the grieving family. Change your visit to a different time of day or a different day. Seeing an open grave may be interesting for older children. It should be done, however, before the graveside service begins.

Some suggestions for details to point out to children include different sizes of grave markers or monuments, unusually shaped monuments, individual mausoleums, a community mausoleum, urns of ashes, varying epitaphs, decorations, flat markers, dates, religious symbols, or words used. Let children walk around and see the differences. You might ask them to find an example of some of the items listed above. Or ask them to find the marker or epitaph that they like best. After you've explored, sit awhile and talk. Let children direct the discussion. Write down any questions you don't know the answer to and get the answers for children later.

Reinforce the lesson by closing with a description of different types of burials, markers, and epitaphs. Remind children that these reflect personal and religious decisions that people have made. The variety represents the great variety of individuals who are buried in the cemetery. The type of burial is an honor to the individual who is buried and represents the individual's beliefs and wishes.

What Do You See on the News?

The main purpose of this strategy is to show children that *death is a part of our lives*. It's important, therefore, to learn about what happens when people die. If you want to extend the activity, you can go into more detail about news articles focusing on facts. The activity is designed for children in the stages typical of ages six through eight and ages nine and over.

Tell children to look through a newspaper, listen to the radio, or watch the evening news. Ask them to look for stories that show a death or a loss and use death-related words when they're not really referring to death. When you make this assignment, take some time to talk about some examples they might find. Have older children make a list of the stories and words they found. Ask younger children to remember two stories to share in class. Parents or caregivers may review newspapers or the news with children at home. Children and adults could make a list together and discuss it when finished.

In the classroom, on the following day, have children present their stories and words to the class. Make a list of their stories on newsprint or the board. Referring to your completed list, make the point that death and loss are a part of our daily lives. Note that we would find just as many stories on any day of the week. Although we are fortunate not to have to deal with personal sadness on a daily basis, we need to know that death and loss are a real part of life.

If you want to extend the lesson, you have some options. You might start by stating that because death is part of our lives, we need to know what happens when a person dies. This statement can lead you to a discussion about beliefs or funeral rituals. Another extension would discuss the cause of deaths and losses in the news. You could identify which causes are preventable and which are not. Or you could focus on various actions people take when a death or loss occurs.

Regardless of your approach, the overall theme is that while death and loss are extremely emotional and often quite sad, they are still part of our lives. We need to learn how to get and give comfort and understand related events. In this way, we learn that life goes on after death and loss.

Funeral Home Visit

This strategy is designed for children in the stages typical of ages six through eight and ages nine and over who have had some experience or background education in the area of death. It is not designed for inexperienced teachers or students. It is an excellent strategy as an *advanced* part of a death education curriculum. It also may be helpful for parents or caregivers to take a child to visit a funeral home to get help with answers to their child's questions. Or if there is a death in the family, a visit prior to the funeral may help a child be prepared for the funeral or visitation. A visit to a funeral home will help children learn the *physical facts* about what a funeral home looks like and what happens there. Also, it may increase their comfort level and decrease anxiety many people feel at the thought of going to a funeral home.

If you're a teacher taking a group of students, you'll need to follow your school district guidelines for field trips. In addition to getting consent for children to travel, it's important to let parents and caregivers know the purpose of the trip, what children will be seeing, and how they will be cared for during the visit.

The way you prepare a child for this type of visit will have a great impact on how successful the visit is for everyone. First, visit the funeral home by yourself. Talk to the person who will be talking to the children. Find out whether the funeral home has any children's programs or if any staff have experience or training working with children. If they do, that's great. If they don't, you may have to prepare the funeral director for how to talk to children in general. Giving the director a sampling of questions your children may ask is a good approach. If you're uncomfortable with the way the staff handles any questions, visit other funeral homes until you find one that you would consider a positive experience.

Before the tour, be sure to establish what the tour will and won't include. For example, you may want to include the embalming room for children in the stage typical for children ages nine and over, but not those in the stage typical of ages six through eight. The area where new coffins are stored is another place you may or may not want to visit. Just being in the funeral home may be enough for a first visit.

As children get older, become more experienced, or have more questions, they will want to see more parts of the facility. Talk to older children to discover their interests. Make sure children know they have a choice about how much they see. For younger children, clearly explain what it will be like on the tour. Tell them who will talk to them and what they will see. Tell them what type of furnishings they'll see. Tell them what rooms they won't see. Most important, assure them that they *won't* see a dead body. Ask children to write down questions they would like to ask. This list will help prepare you and the funeral home guide.

Be sure you have plenty of adult chaperones available for this type of field trip. You may have to divide the group at some time. For example, while some children may want to see coffins, others won't. Children should not be forced. You may need extra adults to supervise children who don't want to see everything the funeral director offers.

Prepare children for contingencies. You may have scheduled your visit ahead of time. If the funeral home has a funeral to conduct, your visit may be canceled. Some children may feel prepared and then have different feelings when they are actually there. Talk with the children ahead of time about what do you do if they change their minds about going with one group, if they feel sad, if they feel like laughing, and so on. Encourage children to speak up and then reassure them. "Since there will be no mourners at the funeral home at the time of our visit, you won't offend anyone if you laugh. If you feel sad, for whatever reason, it's OK. If you change your mind, say so and you can return to the group in the waiting area."

Once you're in the funeral home, with plenty of supportive adults and well-prepared children, let the funeral home guide take over. He or she will talk about the jobs and the facility, just like a field trip to another place of business. Your job is to watch children to see that they're understanding the information and handling the situation. You may need to clarify a child's question or clarify the staff person's response. If children are too shy to ask their questions, you might want to ask questions they gave you in class. Act assertively to help the guide address children's interests and keep the discussion at their level of understanding.

Follow-up after the visit is critical. Be sure to give children plenty of time to ask more questions. If you don't know the answers, write down questions and ask the funeral director or guide. Although this discussion is focused on learning facts, you should let children express whatever ideas or feelings were aroused by the visit. You may ask them to write about their visit or draw something to get more clues as to whether they fully understood and whether they have any misconceptions.

In addition to clarifying facts about what happens in a funeral home, your discussion should reinforce the concept that death is a natural part of life and that what they learned at the visit is what happens, physically, when someone dies.

Teaching Strategies about Beliefs

Compare Beliefs and Rituals

This strategy is designed to introduce children to the concept that people have different death-related beliefs and rituals. It is best suited to give children in the stages typical of ages three through five and ages six through eight. This strategy provides children practice in *expressing* their own beliefs and *identifying* beliefs and rituals that are different from their own. When preparing for this activity, you may want to read about beliefs and practices of other cultures. (See the references and additional readings list at the end of this book.)

Read two stories to children that include different cultural, religious, or spiritual beliefs and practices related to death. (Refer to list of books included in the last section of this chapter.) Ask children to help you make a list of beliefs and practices described in each story. Then discuss and compare beliefs and practices in the two stories. To continue the strategy, ask children if they know of other practices that weren't included in the stories. When you close the activity, remember to stress the variety of practices and the comfort provided by beliefs and practices.

Interview Your Family

This strategy will help children see how their families' *backgrounds determine* their beliefs. It is most appropriate for children in the stages typical of ages six through eight and ages nine and over. In formal settings, you may want to prepare a letter to parents explaining the assignment. Be sure parents know that beliefs are not going to be evaluated, just discussed. Some children may need to find a neighbor or adult friend to interview if their parents or caregivers are unavailable.

Tell children you want to find out about all the different beliefs people have related to death. Ask them to help you come up with a list of questions for which you'd all like to know answers. Have children take the list of questions home and interview an adult. When the interviews are completed, ask children to share their results with the class. Stress the variety of beliefs and practices and how our culture and religion help us decide what's right for us. You could adapt the strategy by having children interview their families regarding experiences, feelings, or any other concept related to death or loss.

As you end the strategy, suggest that children reflect on their own beliefs. Have them write a descriptive paragraph or answer some of the following questions in discussion or writing: Were any of your family member's answers new to you? Did you hear any different views in class that were interesting to you? How did you feel about beliefs that were different from yours or those of your family? What do you believe at this moment?

Death in Different Cultures

This strategy challenges children in the stage typical of ages nine and over to explore the death-related beliefs of *different cultures.* Begin with your child's regular social studies book. Whether studying Native Americans or ancient or world cultures, take time to look at the way those cultures view or viewed death. If your current text doesn't include references to death, look through some older social studies texts or the list of references and additional readings at the end of this book.

Ask children to tell you what they know about ways people deal with death. What happens to the body? What is a funeral like? How is burial done? What do people do when they grieve? What differences do they know about in our culture? Do they know how Native Americans or ancient Egyptians dealt with death? Since they're not likely to know much about this, design a research assignment. To create interest in this activity, describe a Viking funeral pyre set out to sea. Children often find this exciting.

Divide the topic by culture (Native American, Roman, and so on) or by part of the ritual (preparation of the body, burial, processions, eulogy, and so on). Let children work in groups on different parts of this assignment. In addition to textbooks, you will find this type of information in some nonfiction children's books about death and dying or on the internet. If you think your children will have trouble finding material, consider bringing items to class for them (for example, old social studies texts, nonfiction children's books, biographies, and past and present newspapers).

You can extend this idea to compare information in obituaries today and those printed at the turn of the century. Use biographies to find out about the funerals of famous people like U.S. presidents or Roman leaders or Chinese emperors. Then make comparisons.

When research is done, in formal settings, have children present their material to the class orally. Make a chart on the board comparing different cultures. Talk about why certain cultures may believe or do what they do. Is it related to religious or spiritual beliefs? Is it because of limited knowledge? Is it because of fear? Is it because of environmental or social issues? What else do you know about the culture that might affect beliefs and rituals related to death?

In closing, reinforce the idea that differences in the way people deal with death are the result of their broader culture. These traditions and rituals aren't good or bad, they're just different and often are quite interesting.

Teaching Strategies about Feelings

Finish the Sentence

This strategy is appropriate for children in the stages typical of ages six through eight and ages nine and over because of the need for reading skills. You also could complete this strategy orally with small groups of children in the stage typical of ages three through five. Depending on the focus you choose, this strategy is designed to help you understand what children feel or know. Also, it gives children the chance to practice expressing their feelings, think about other's views, learn some new facts, or any combination of these things.

After you decide whether you want to focus on feelings or knowledge, develop a list of open-ended questions. Prepare a written handout of your questions. Before you present the activity to the class, try filling in the sentences yourself. Write your own answers as well as some possible children's responses.

Give children a list of incomplete sentences with blank spaces at the end. For example: When I watch a television show about a divorce, I feel _____. Ask children to fill in the blanks in each sentence by describing their feelings. Divide children into pairs or small groups to discuss their answers before you discuss them with the whole group, listing various responses on the board or a newsprint pad.

In another variation, you would substitute factual sentences for feeling sentences. For example: When a dead body is cremated, it is _____. The number of open-ended statements you use will depend on time available for the activity and abilities of the children. Select statements either that are most appropriate for your children's stage and interest or that focus on your teaching goal.

As you end the activity, remember to provide positive reinforcement for children's participation. Note the variety of responses and wealth of knowledge or compassion they have about the subject. As long as none of the feelings mentioned include responsibility for a death, be sure to maintain your open environment, accepting and respecting all feelings. Conclude with a clear statement about all feelings being OK and the importance of sharing them.

Feelings in Children's Stories

The following strategies are most appropriate for children in the stages typical of ages three through five and ages six through eight. These strategies are designed to give children *practice in expressing* their feelings and thinking about how others might feel.

Read a children's story that includes examples of death- or loss-related situations. (Refer to the list of references and additional readings at the end of this book.) Ask children to listen to how different characters feel about what happened. Follow the story with a discussion of how feelings were presented in the story. How did you know what characters felt? Was it from pictures, expressions, words, or something else? Then ask children to tell how they might feel if this happened to them.

If this type of activity is difficult or uncomfortable for children, start the discussion by sharing how you would feel. Sharing your feelings can be important as long as you make sure children know that everyone's feelings are important and accepted. Remember to think like a child, realizing that children will have varying degrees of ability to think about another person or character.

Further follow-up could include an art activity in which children are asked to make a picture or collage showing a feeling like one of the characters felt or showing how they would feel if they were one of the characters. Be sure to collect the artwork and display it.

When working with younger children, use paper cutouts or puppets to represent characters in the story. Prepare a large three-column chart with feeling words at the top or varied faces like "smiley," "neutral," and "frowny." Then, as you discuss characters' feelings, have children match the paper dolls or puppets with the feeling.

Depending on your discussion, you can explore how one character feels different emotions throughout the story or how different characters feel different emotions. Either way, stress the variety of acceptable feelings. You also could designate areas of the room as different feelings. Then as you name feelings, children can reflect on their own feelings and place themselves physically in the area that represents that feeling. This is a way to let children reflect and see how

Using Planned Learning Strategies

other children feel about the same story without having to verbalize their thoughts or feelings.

Regardless of the specific approach you take, end the activity by stressing the variety of acceptable feelings. Include some supportive closing concepts suggested earlier.

Video Activities

Videos can be used for children in almost all stages. Just vary the length and follow-up strategies to fit the developmental abilities of the children. Some of the tips about using children's literature also apply to selecting and using videos.

Select a video with examples of death or loss situations. Without giving away information that might spoil the story for them, prepare them for the possibility of sadness or discomfort, if necessary.

After the video, ask some specific questions about the feelings or actions in the story. Your questions should help children focus on the issues you want to discuss in your follow-up strategies. Follow the video by clarifying the story line. Then discuss the feelings as described in the previous activity.

You can vary this strategy by focusing on coping skills. For younger children, ask them to make sympathy cards for characters in the video who experienced the death or loss. You may need to provide some sample sympathy cards and phrases if these are unfamiliar to children. Be sure children understand not to copy the samples. Encourage them to express their own feelings and ideas. For older children, have them conduct a pretend funeral for the character who died in the video. Follow descriptions of the pretend funeral activity at the end of this chapter.

All My Feelings Count

The purpose of this strategy is to help young children in the stages typical of ages under three and ages three through five understand the *importance and variety* of acceptable feelings and to provide them with some practice at recognizing their feelings.

To prepare for this strategy, you'll need a group of pictures, pieces of music, or smells that you think will arouse children's feelings. You'll also need to make "feeling cards." These may have colors; words; or smiling, neutral, and frowning faces. The cards could even be heart-shaped. Review each feeling card to be sure children understand what feeling the card represents.

Begin this activity by giving each child a paper bag and a selection of feeling cards. Ask children to decorate the bag by drawing a picture of themselves on their bag. Then tell them, "Today we're going to find out how music, pictures, and smells can make us feel things." For each piece of music, picture, or smell presented to children, ask them to think for a bit, then choose a card that shows how music or pictures make them feel. Children will keep their collection of feeling cards in their own bags.

Remind children that each person has many different feelings at different times. A feeling doesn't stay with a person all the time. If you're feeling sad, sometimes a happy song will make you happy. Or if you're angry, a funny picture will make you laugh. Sometimes our feelings affect how we act. Sometimes we're too sad to play, and sometimes we're too excited to work on lessons.

As you end the strategy, have children look through all their feeling cards. They can even count them. Can they remember some of their feelings? Consider having children share their bag of feelings with their families.

Teaching Strategies about Coping Skills

Memory Show-and-Tell

The purpose of this strategy is to help children learn to express and listen to sensitive feelings. It can be adapted to use at any stage of development. In this scenario, children are asked to talk about something from their past, not a current death or loss. The idea is for children to get some practice sharing feelings when a particular death or loss is not traumatic currently. You may need to give children an example to help them understand the assignment.

Ask children to bring in an object or story that reminds them of something they've lost or someone who has died. Sit in a circle to make the sharing time more intimate. Tell children, "Today we're going to take turns telling about our memories of something we have lost or someone who has died." Ask for volunteers to tell their stories. Encourage all the children to share their feelings, but don't force anyone to share.

Depending on the developmental stage of the children, you'll need to vary content. Younger children may remember an activity or toy they miss or a more significant loss. Children in the middle stages may deal with dead pets or people. Older children may think about many of these. Another variation is to have older children share rituals they have observed.

If you're doing this assignment at school or in a formal setting, you will want to send a note to parents and caregivers about the assignment. Describe the activity and what you hope the children will learn from it. Give parents and caregivers some examples of what you have in mind for show-and-tell so they can help any children who may have difficulty with the assignment. Your note also could include a suggestion that parents discuss memories with their children before and after the school activity.

If you think children may become sad or cry, ask another trusted adult to be nearby when you do these activities. This may not be necessary, but you need to be prepared to provide support that children might need.

The emphasis of this strategy is that all our feelings are important to us and that sharing feelings is helpful. However, if a child expresses the feeling of responsibility for a natural death or loss, remember to treat this feeling differently. You must tell the child that it was not his or her fault. Be alert to this possibility as children share their stories.

As children put away their mementos, explain that sometimes people also put away their feelings: "You can put away a hurtful feeling for a while if it starts to hurt too much. Or if you feel especially sad about someone or something you're missing, you can take out a special memory you have put away and let the memory help you feel better."

Pretend Funeral

This strategy is best suited for children in the stages typical of ages six through eight and ages nine and over. It could be simplified for children in the stage typical of ages three through five as well. The focus is on learning about rituals by planning a pretend funeral.

Depending on the developmental stage of the children, you'll need to provide more or less structure for this activity. Older children may identify tasks and distribute them to specific work groups by themselves. Younger children will probably need work groups identified and to be given a list of things to do. Children in the middle stage may benefit from the comfort of preestablished work groups, but let them decide on the specific tasks of each group. Start by offering broad suggestions and getting more specific until you feel children are ready to begin action on their own.

If you're uncomfortable with this type of activity, it's not right for you. Review chapter 1, or wait until you develop more experience or have the right group of students to handle the activity. If you think your students won't take it seriously, they're probably not ready for it either. But this activity can be appropriate and beneficial for some children, especially if there's been a series of other death education activities as preparation.

Tell children they are going to plan a pretend funeral for a stuffed toy or a character in a story or movie. Divide the children into small groups and assign a specific part of the funeral arrangements to each group. For example, they can focus on funeral home arrangements, music, memorials, burial, eulogy, and decorations. You may need to work with each group to help them come up with a list of tasks.

You also could provide a checklist of tasks for each group. The funeral home group would plan the time of the funeral, the clothing or other preparation of body, the casket, the casket lining, and visitation. The burial group plans cemetery, grave, and tombstone. The eulogy group decides on the service, what should be said, and how the funeral is to be conducted. The decorations group's tasks might include deciding on flowers and music and planning a reception after the service.

If children come from varied cultural or religious or spiritual backgrounds, the pretend funeral may be a mixed version. It doesn't matter. Let children come up with whatever they feel is appropriate. When closing the activity, remember to stress the variety of rituals that people follow and how these actions and rituals often provide comfort.

Choosing and Using Children's Literature

Even when children are developmentally able to think about abstract concepts, hands-on activities still may make the greatest impact. In the case of death education, where real examples can't be simulated, the next best option for parents, caregivers, and teachers is to use literature. Children's literature can provide situations or scenarios likely to elicit reactions similar to what might occur in a real-life experience.

You must do more than preview your materials. Make sure you know the video or book content, dialogue, and images very well. When you're previewing, pay attention to the particular details you want to focus on. Be aware of any feelings that might be aroused in the children or yourself. Identify any information that might present a biased view. Biased material might still be useful provided you're aware of the slant and can compensate for it.

Since children will surprise you with their responses, consider as many possible responses as you can. If you feel you need more background information to tackle an activity, use the references and additional readings at the back of the book to help you with your research.

The rest of this chapter offers suggestions for selecting appropriate children's literature and using it effectively, including a list of some children's books by topic focus.

When choosing literature for use in death education, think about the following points:

- whether the age level is appropriate,
- whether you want fiction or nonfiction,
- whether the approach of the story fits your purpose,
- whether you want a focused or comprehensive story, and
- whether the book presents a positive view of death.

Select an Age-Appropriate Book

Remember to consider the age and developmental level of children in regard to their understanding of death. Because of our societal taboos, this developmental level may be lower than their developmental level in math or science. As you review each book, try to think from the child's perspective. Then prepare to bring the discussion level up or down depending on responses you anticipate from children. At this step, look for appropriate language. Only language that is direct and honest is acceptable. (Refer to the table on direct, meaningful language in chapter 4.)

For purposes of this chapter, books are recommended for just two general stages: that typical of children ages three through five and that typical of ages six through eight. Children ages nine and over may be reading and choosing books on their own. They also can benefit from any of the books recommended for the stage typical of children ages six through eight.

There really are no books aimed at children under three. When these youngest children experience a death, they are likely to jump ahead developmentally with regard to understanding. When death is a reality in their lives, you'll be able to use some of the books for the three- through five-year-olds to help comfort and teach them. Stories that work best are those that are simple and most like the actual situation the child is experiencing.

Decide on Fiction or Nonfiction

Fiction will work best in most situations. Whether you're presenting a planned classroom unit on death education or preparing a child for an expected death in the family, using a fictional story to develop scenarios often will draw out children's feelings, knowledge, and beliefs. A story will help children cope with a death experience if it shows the range of common feelings and responses to help children feel more "normal" and comfortable with their own reactions.

Nonfiction books on death and dying are probably more useful for adults than for children. Because these books often focus only on technical details, children who are less experienced with the concept of death may find this somewhat detached approach too harsh or blunt. Although emotions may be discussed, they often are presented as generic or abstract instead of personal and meaningful. In most cases, a more sympathetic (that is, personal, human, real-life, realistic) approach will be desirable, even when the child's questions focus on factual details.

In addition, nonfiction books about death tend to cover too much material. They may present too many steps for children to understand at one time. Many nonfiction books can be useful to adults, however, by providing background material on the subject of death at varying levels of detail. They also provide excellent models for direct language to be used with children at different levels.

Examples of nonfiction books for children in the stage typical of ages three through five:

- *A Look at Death,* by Rebecca Anders
- *Sunny: The Death of a Pet,* by Judith E. Greenberg and Helen H. Carey
- *When a Pet Dies,* by Fred Rogers

Examples of nonfiction books for children in the stage typical of ages six through eight:

- *When People Die,* by Joanne E. Bernstein and Stephen V. Gullo
- *When Dinosaurs Die: A Guide to Understanding Death,* by Laurie K. Brown and Marc Brown
- *Let's Talk about Going to a Funeral,* by Marianne Johnston
- *Death and Dying,* by Jean Knox
- *When Someone You Love Dies,* by Linda L. Potter
- *What on Earth Do You Do When Someone Dies?* by Trevor Romain
- *Death Customs,* by Lucy Rushton
- *Let's Talk about When a Parent Dies,* by Elizabeth Weitzman

Consider the Book's Approach

Authors of children's books approach the subject of death in various ways. Death may be the main theme of the book, or it may be a secondary theme—with less emphasis placed on it. Some books take a natural or biological approach to the subject of death, while others use metaphors or fantasy. When a book deals directly with a specific death, some authors have chosen to write about the death of a grandparent, while others write about the death of a parent, child, or pet.

When you're choosing a book to read to children, consider which approach will be most helpful. You may precede a death education unit with a story in which death is a secondary theme. This format may help you judge children's knowledge and emotional responses to the subject while helping you plan lessons directed more accurately at your children's level of understanding. The list of books for children at the end of this book all have death as the primary theme.

Books taking a natural or biological approach to death typically use the seasons of nature to describe the natural flow of life and death. An author will emphasize the fact that death is a natural and necessary part of life. For the stage typical of children ages three through five, the book *Lifetimes: The Beautiful Way to Explain Death to Children,* by B. Melonie and R. Ingpen, tells this story simply and directly. *The Tenth Good Thing about Barney,* by Judith Viorst, is an example of a book that is helpful until the end where it describes the buried pet as nourishment for new growth. For most children younger than nine, the principle of decomposition is difficult to understand, thus creating confusion about the facts. If you can clarify or if you know your children understand this principle, then this book will work. Otherwise, you would omit the ending or select another book.

For children in the stage typical of ages six through eight, *The Fall of Freddie the Leaf, by* Leo Buscaglia, and *Death Is Natural,* by Laurence Pringle, teach this lesson well. Buscaglia tells the story of Freddie, a leaf with lifelike qualities and thoughts. This popular and easy-to-find book has a clever, fun-to-read, positive attitude toward death. Adults may have to clarify some of the facts and metaphors used. Dying is referred to as changing homes, not hurting, and being more comfortable. In the context of the book, these metaphors all make sense to an adult reader. Children may need some help understanding. Descriptions of afterlife, while positive and interesting, may require some interpretation for children. Pringle presents general feelings and beliefs about death in an ecological-primer style. Life cycles, nature's balance, and natural selection are emphasized. Books with this approach can be used effectively to initiate general discussions about death.

Although metaphors such as people living on in our memories often are difficult for children to understand before age nine, some authors use them rather effectively. Before you use such a metaphorical story, you should be very familiar with the abilities of your children and very comfortable personally with the specific metaphor used. If you are unsure about a story, either avoid using it or spend sufficient time discussing the metaphor to clarify its meaning for children.

Using Planned Learning Strategies

If you think your children will enjoy and understand this kind of story, the following books are good examples:

- *First Snow,* by Helen Coutant
- *The Last Leaf,* by O. Henry
- *Annie and the Old One,* by Miska Miles

Some authors write about a specific death experience. When you are working with children who currently are experiencing a death in their lives, choose a children's story in which the real experience and the story experience are similar. If you want to discuss the death of a pet, here are some examples:

- *The Accident,* by Carol Carrick
- *Maggie and Silky and Joe,* by Amy Ehrlich
- *Mustard,* by Charlotte Graeber
- *Better with Two,* by Barbara M. Joosse
- *Goodbye, Max,* by Holly Keller
- *Whiskers Once and Always,* by Doris Orgel
- *Growing Time,* by Sandol S. Warburg

These books deal with the death of a grandparent:

- *My Grandpa Died Today,* by Joan Fassler
- *Grandpa's Slide Show,* by Deborah Gould
- *Why Did Grandpa Die?* by Barbara S. Hazen
- *My Grandmother Died—But I Won't Forget Her,* by Bernice Hogan
- *Why Did Grandma Die?* by Trudy Madler
- *Bubby, Me, and Memories,* by Barbara Pomerantz
- *When Grandpa Died,* by Margaret Stevens
- *My Grandson Lew,* by Charlotte Zolotow

These books are about the death of a parent or teacher:

- *It's Okay to Cry,* by Leone C. Anderson
- *Everett Anderson's Goodbye,* by Lucille Clifton

- *Z's Gift,* by Neal Starkman
- *Saying Goodbye to Daddy,* by Judith Vigna
- *Let's Talk about When a Parent Dies,* by Elizabeth Weitzman

And these stories deal with the death of a child:

- *I Had a Friend Named Peter: Talking to Children about the Death of a Friend,* by Janice Cohn
- *The Magic Moth,* by Virginia Lee
- *We Remember Philip,* by Norma Simon
- *The Saddest Time—Part Two,* by Norma Simon
- *A Taste of Blackberries,* by Doris B. Smith

Think about the Focus of the Book

Your last consideration when choosing a book for children is whether you want a story that is focused on one specific death education concept or whether you want a story that covers the concepts comprehensively. If you already know your children's abilities well, you might know that you need to focus on facts, feelings, beliefs, or coping skills related to death. If you're fishing for clues to your children's understanding, you might decide to present a comprehensive story to see what area children are most interested in or where they need clarification. A comprehensive book will take longer to discuss because there will be more concepts presented in the story.

Assure a Positive View of Death

Finally, you *must* make sure that the overall content of the book presents a positive view of death that promotes the healthy emotional development of children. Remember from chapter 1 that a positive view of death:

- is factually accurate,
- is appropriate for the child's level of understanding, and
- creates a healthy understanding of death as a natural part of life rather than promoting fear and misunderstanding.

As you preview each book, look at both words and images. Both words and images should be positive, providing appropriate responses to questions and feelings that are expressed by characters in the story. And once again, all language must be direct and honest.

Glossary
References and Additional Readings

Glossary

Afterlife. Existence after death.

Animism. Attribution of life to inanimate objects, often occurring in the developmental stage typical of children ages three through five.

Ashes. Remains of a dead body after cremation.

Bereaved. Suffering from the death of a loved one.

Burial permit. Legal document necessary before burying a body.

Casket. Box for burying a dead body.

Cemetery. Burial ground.

Committal. Graveside service, including burial.

Cremains. Ashes of a cremated body.

Cremation. Process used to reduce a dead body to ashes by burning; it may be an alternative to burial, or ashes may be buried.

Crepe. Fabric worn or draped on a doorway as a sign of mourning.

Crypt. Room used as a burial place, often underground.

Death concepts. Ways a person views death; these develop with increased understanding and include the ideas that death is:

Avoidable—Can be escaped;

Final—Not reversible;

Impersonal—Can't happen to me or loved ones;

Inevitable—Happens to everyone eventually;

Personal—Can happen to me and my loved ones;

Reversible—Changeable or temporary;

Universal—Same as inevitable.

Decomposition. Process of a body decaying.

Egocentrism. Inability to consider another's viewpoint, often occurring in the developmental stage typical of children ages three through five.

Embalming. Treatment of a dead body to sanitize it for viewing.

Entombment. Burial in a mausoleum.

Epitaph. Words written on a grave marker or monument.

Eulogy. Speech of praise for a dead person.

Euphemism. A less direct word substituted for one that is thought to be offensive.

Funeral service. Ceremonies held for the dead before burial or cremation.

Grave. Hole in the ground for burying a body.

Grief. Extreme distress caused by bereavement.

Hearse. Vehicle for taking the dead to the grave.

Heaven. Religious term for the place the blessed dead exist in communion with God.

Hell. Religious term for the place where the damned dead exist in continual punishment.

Immortality. Being exempt from death.

Interment. Burial.

Kaddish. Jewish prayer recited after death of a friend or relative.

Last rites. Religious rituals to ease the transition from life to death.

Magical thinking. Belief that objects and people have power to make other people do things, occurring in the developmental stage typical of children ages three through five.

Mausoleum. Building for above-ground burials.

Memorial service. Ceremony conducted after the burial or when the dead body is not present.

Metaphor. A figure of speech in which one thing is spoken of as if it were another.

Monument. Stone placed on a grave to memorialize the dead.

Mortuary. Place where dead bodies are kept until burial.

Mourning. Outward signs of grief or bereavement.

Negative presentation of death. View of death that is factually inaccurate, that is not appropriate for the developmental level of the child, that creates unhealthy fears of life and death, or that is any combination of these things.

Obituary. Notice of a person's death, usually in a newspaper or periodical.

Pall. Heavy cloth draped over a casket.

Pallbearer. Person who helps carry a casket at a funeral and burial.

Positive presentation of death. View that is factually accurate, that is appropriate for the developmental level of the child, and that creates a healthy understanding of death as a part of life.

Reincarnation. Religious concept of rebirth into a new body or life form.

Restoration. Making the dead body look as close as possible to lifelike for viewing.

Resurrection. Religious concept of rising from the dead.

Resuscitation. Medical intervention to revive a person from apparent death or unconsciousness.

Shiva. Jewish ritual of seven days of formal mourning after the funeral of a close relative.

Shroud. Cloth or ritual garments in which a body is wrapped when buried.

Soul. Spiritual concept of the essence of an individual.

Thanatology. The study of death and dying.

Urn. Container used for keeping ashes of the dead.

Vault. Concrete (or other strong material)functioning as a lining for a grave.

Viewing. Physical display of a dead person at the funeral home or chapel.

Visitation. Same as viewing.

Wake. Christian watch over the dead body prior to the funeral, similar to visitation.

References and Additional Readings

Sources for Adults
Books for Children
Internet Sources

The foundation of our research comes from classic sources because they withstand the test of time very well. Our suggested readings, however, have been updated to include resources with more current examples, applications, and illustrations.

Sources for Adults

Bernstein, J. E. 1977. *Books to Help Children Cope with Separation and Loss.* New York: R. R. Bowker.

Corr, C. A., C. M. Nabe, and D. M. Corr. 1997. *Death and Dying, Life and Living.* Pacific Grove, CA: Brooks/Cole.

Deaton, R. L., and W. A. Berkan. 1995. *Planning and Managing Death Issues in the Schools: A Handbook.* Westport, CT: Greenwood.

DeSpelder, L. A., and A. L. Strickland. 1999. *The Last Dance: Encountering Death and Dying.* Mountain View, CA: Mayfield.

Doka, K. J. 1995. *Children Mourning, Mourning Children.* Washington, DC: Hospice Foundation of America.

Doka, K. J., and J. D. Davidson, eds. 1998. *Living with Grief.* Washington, DC: Hospice Foundation of America.

Eddy, J. M., and W. F. Alles. 1983. *Death Education.* St. Louis: C. V. Mosby.

Elkind, D. 1977. Life and Death: Concepts and Feelings in Children. *Day Care and Early Childhood Education* 4(3):27–29, 39.

Garanzini, M. J. 1987. Explaining Death to Children: The Healing Process. *Momentum* 18(4):30–32.

Goldman, L. 1994. *Life and Loss. A Guide to Help Grieving Children.* Bristol, PA: Accelerated Development.

————. 1996. *Breaking the Silence: A Guide to help Children with Complicated Grief, Suicide, Homicide, AIDS, Violence, and Abuse.* Bristol, PA: Accelerated Development.

Grollman, E. 1967. *Explaining Death to Children.* Boston: Beacon.

————. 1970. *Talking to Children about Death.* Boston: Beacon.

Hardt, D. V. 1979. *Death: The Final Frontier.* Englewood Cliffs, NJ: Prentice-Hall.

Kastenbaum, R., and R. Aisenberg. 1976. *The Psychology of Death.* New York: Springer.

Ketchel, J. A. 1986. Helping the Young Child Cope with Death. *Day Care and Early Education* 14(2):24–27.

Kübler-Ross, E. 1969. *On Death and Dying.* New York: Macmillan.

————. 1975. *Death: The Final Stage of Growth.* Englewood Cliffs, NJ: Prentice-Hall.

————. 1983. *On Children and Death.* New York: Macmillan.

Mendler, A. N. 1990. *Smiling at Yourself.* Santa Cruz, CA: ETR Associates.

Oehlberg, B. 1996. *Making It Better: Activities for Children Living in a Stressful World.* St. Paul, MN: Redleaf.

Ordal, C. C. 1980. Death as Seen in Books for Young Children. *Death Education* 4:223–36.

Papadatou, D., and C. Papadatou, eds. 1991. *Children and Death.* New York: Taylor and Francis.

Piaget, J. 1983. *The Child's Conception of the World.* Totowa, NJ: Rowan and Allanheld.

Pratt, C. C., J. Hare, and C. Wright. 1987. Death and Dying in Early Childhood Education: Are Educators Prepared? *Education* 107:279–86.

Russell, R. D., and C. O. Purdy. 1980. *Coping with Death and Dying.* Glenview, IL: Scott, Foresman.

Speece, M. W., and S. B. Brent. 1984. Children's Understanding of Death: A Review of Three Components of a Death Concept. *Child Development* 55:1671–86.

Stevenson, R. B., ed. 1995. *What Will We Do? Preparing a School Community to Cope with Crisis.* Amityville, NY: Baywood.

Stevenson, R. G., and E. P. Stevenson, eds. 1996. *Teaching Students about Death.* Philadelphia: Charles.

Sutherland, S. 2000. *Good Grief: Helping Groups of Children When a Friend Dies.* Boston: The New England Association for the Education of Young Children.

Wass, H., and C. A. Corr. 1982. *Helping Children Cope with Death: Guidelines and Resources.* Washington, DC: Hemisphere.

Wass, H., and J. Shaake. 1976. Helping Children Understand Death Through Literature. *Childhood Education* 53:80–85.

Webb, N. B., ed. 1993. *Helping Bereaved Children: A Handbook for Practitioners.* New York: Guilford.

Wenestam, C. G., and H. Wass. 1987. Swedish and U. S. Children's Thinking about Death: A Qualitative Study and Cross-Cultural Comparison. *Death Studies* 11:99–121.

Wolfelt, A. 1983. *Helping Children Cope with Grief.* Muncie, IN: Accelerated Development.

Books for Children

Anders, R. 1978. *A Look at Death.* Minneapolis: Lerner.

Anderson, L. C. 1979. *It's Okay to Cry.* Elgin, IL: Child's World.

Arecllana, F. 1999. *The Mats.* Brooklyn: Kane/Miller.

Bernstein, J. E., and S. V. Gullo. 1977. *When People Die.* New York: Dutton.

Boulden, J. 1989. *Saying Goodbye.* Santa Rosa, CA: Boulden.

Brown, L. K., and M. Brown. 1996. *When Dinosaurs Die. A Guide to Understanding Death.* Boston: Little, Brown.

Buscaglia, L. 1982. *The Fall of Freddie the Leaf.* Thorofare, NJ: Slack.

Carrick, C. 1976. *The Accident.* New York: Seabury.

Clifton, L. 1983. *Everett Anderson's Goodbye.* New York: Holt, Rinehart, and Winston.

Cohn, J. 1987. *I Had a Friend Named Peter: Talking to Children about the Death of a Friend.* New York: Morrow.

———. 1994. *Molly's Rosebush.* Morton Grove, IL: Albert Whitman.

———. 1994. *Why Did It Happen? Helping Children Cope in a Violent World.* New York: Morrow.

Coutant, H. 1974. *First Snow.* New York: Knopf.

Ehrlich, A. 1994. *Maggie and Silky and Joe.* New York: Viking.

Fassler, J. 1971. *My Grandpa Died Today.* New York: Human Sciences.

Gould, D. 1987. *Grandpa's Slide Show.* New York: Lothrop, Lee, and Shepard.

Graeber, C. 1982. *Mustard.* New York: Bantam.

Greenberg, J. E., and H. H. Carey. 1986. *Sunny: The Death of a Pet.* New York: Franklin Watts.

Hazen, B. S. 1985. *Why Did Grandpa Die?* New York: Golden.

Henkes, Kevin. 1997. *Sun and Spoon.* New York: Puffin.

Henry, O. [W. S. Porter]. 1980. *The Last Leaf.* Mankato, MN: Creative Education.

Hogan, B. 1983. *My Grandmother Died—But I Won't Forget Her.* Nashville: Abingdon.

Johnston, M. 1998. *Let's Talk about Going to a Funeral.* New York: Rosen.

Joosse, B. M. 1988. *Better with Two.* Singapore: HarperCollins.

———. 2001. *Ghost Wings.* San Francisco: Chronicle.

Keller, H. 1987. *Goodbye, Max.* New York: Greenwillow.

Knox, J. 1989. *Death and Dying.* New York: Chelsea.

Lee, V. 1972. *The Magic Moth.* New York: Houghton Mifflin.

Madenski, Melissa. 1991. *Some of the Pieces.* Boston: Little, Brown.

Madler, T. 1980. *Why Did Grandma Die?* Milwaukee: Raintree.

Mellonie, B., and R. Ingpen. *Lifetimes: The Beautiful Way to Explain Death to Children.* New York: Bantam.

Miles, M. 1971. *Annie and the Old One*. Boston: Little, Brown.

Orgel, D. 1986. *Whiskers Once and Always*. New York: Viking.

Pomerantz, B. 1983. *Bubby, Me, and Memories*. New York: Union of American Hebrew Congregations.

Potter, L. L. 1979. *When Someone You Love Dies*. Lincoln, NE: Word Services.

Pringle, L. 1977. *Death Is Natural*. New York: Four Winds.

Rogers, F. 1988. *When a Pet Dies*. New York: Putnam.

Romain, T. 1999. *What on Earth Do You Do When Someone Dies?* Minneapolis: Free Spirit.

Rushton, L. 1998. *Death Customs*. Boston: Thomson Learning.

Simon, N. 1979. *We Remember Philip*. Niles, IL: Albert Whitman.

———. 1986. *The Saddest Time*. Niles, IL: Albert Whitman.

Smith, D. B. 1973. *A Taste of Blackberries*. New York: HarperCollins.

Starkman, N. 1988. *Z's Gift*. Seattle: Comprehensive Health Education Foundation.

Stevens, M. 1979. *When Grandpa Died*. Chicago: Children's.

Vigna, J. 1991. *Saying Goodbye to Daddy*. Morton Grove, IL: Albert Whitman.

Viorst, J. 1971. *The Tenth Good Thing about Barney*. New York: Macmillan.

Warburg, S. S. 1969. *Growing Time*. Boston: Houghton Mifflin.

Weitzman, E. 1996. *Let's Talk about When a Parent Dies*. New York: Rosen.

Zolotow, C. 1974. *My Grandson Lew*. New York: HarperCollins.

Internet Sources

This list of websites is provided as a starting point for your internet searching. It is not comprehensive, yet using the links from these pages will put you in touch with a vast range of topics and perspectives on death and loss.

Association for Death Education and Counseling: www.adec.org

This is a multidisciplinary professional organization dedicated to promoting excellence in death education, bereavement counseling, and care of the dying.

The Compassionate Friends: www.compassionatefriends.org

The mission of the Compassionate Friends is to assist families toward the positive resolution of grief following the death of a child of any age and to provide information to help others be supportive. The Compassionate Friends is a national nonprofit, self-help support organization that offers friendship and understanding to bereaved parents, grandparents, and siblings. There is no religious affiliation and there are no membership dues or fees.

The Dougy Center: www.dougy.org

The Dougy Center was the first center in the United States to provide peer support groups for grieving children. It has served over 13,500 children, teens, and families since 1982. The Dougy Center is a nonprofit organization that is privately supported and does not charge a fee for services.

Growth House: www.growthhouse.org

This website provides resources for life-threatening illness and end-of-life care. Its primary mission is to improve the quality of compassionate care for people who are dying through public education and global professional collaboration.

Helping Children Deal with Grief: www.erols.com/lgold

This site contains detailed information discussing complicated grief stemming from traumatic death, AIDS, abuse, or violence. Workshops by Linda Goldman, teacher, counselor, author, certified grief therapist, and educator, are designed to help parents, educators, and therapists.

Hospice Foundation of America: www.hospicefoundation.org

Hospice Foundation of America is a nonprofit organization that provides leadership in development and application of hospice and its philosophy of care. Through programs of professional development, research, public education, and information, Hospice Foundation of America assists those who cope either personally or professionally with terminal illness, death, and the process of grief.

The National Center for Grieving Children and Families: www.grievingchild.org

This site contains a national directory of children's grief programs and resources for children and adults. It is a service of the Dougy Center.

National Hospice and Palliative Care Organization: www.nhpco.org

The National Hospice and Palliative Care Organization is the largest nonprofit membership organization representing hospice and palliative care programs and professionals in the United States. The organization is committed to improving end-of-life care and expanding access to hospice care with the goal of profoundly enhancing the quality of life for people dying in America and their loved ones.

Renew Center for Personal Recovery: www.renew.net

Specialist in crisis management for schools and other organizations, Renew Center for Personal Recovery offers services to individuals, families, and corporations experiencing any kind of trauma or loss.

Dinah Seibert, a faculty member at Southern Illinois University Carbondale, has dedicated over twenty years to community education, particularly in the areas of hospice care for the terminally ill and death education for young children. She was a founding member of her local hospice organization and developed its volunteer training curriculum. She also has designed and facilitated professional and community workshops for counselors, clergy, parents, teachers, and other community groups. Her primary work involves advocating for children. Seibert has published numerous articles in professional journals.

Judy C. Drolet, a professor of health education at Southern Illinois University Carbondale, has taught courses on mental and emotional health, human growth and development, and death education for over twenty-five years. She has conducted over fifty research and evaluation studies and has published widely in the areas of mental health, sexuality education, professional preparation, and death education.

Joyce V. Fetro, a professor of health education at Southern Illinois University Carbondale, has taught in middle school and worked as a supervisor and health education curriculum specialist for the San Francisco Unified School District. In addition to teaching death education, she has developed classroom strategies for middle and high school students and has conducted professional development sessions for teachers about dealing with death and other losses. She is the author of *Step by Step to Health-Promoting Schools* and *Personal and Social Skills: Levels 1–3*.